MURDER, MADNESS AND MAYHEM

Criminal Insanity in Victorian and Edwardian Britain

MURDER, MADNESS AND MAYHEM

Criminal Insanity in Victorian and Edwardian Britain

Kathryn Burtinshaw and John Burt

PEN & SWORD
HISTORY

First published in Great Britain in 2018 by
PEN AND SWORD HISTORY
an imprint of
Pen and Sword Books Ltd
47 Church Street
Barnsley
South Yorkshire S70 2AS

HB ISBN 978 1 52673 455 6
PB ISBN 978 1 52675 137 9

Printed and bound in the UK by TJ International Ltd,
Padstow, Cornwall

Typeset in Times New Roman 11/13.5 by
Aura Technology and Software Services, India

Pen & Sword Books Ltd incorporates the imprints of Pen & Sword
Archaeology, Atlas, Aviation, Battleground, Discovery,
Family History, History, Maritime, Military, Naval, Politics, Railways,
Select, Social History, Transport, True Crime, Claymore Press,
Frontline Books, Leo Cooper, Praetorian Press, Remember When,
Seaforth Publishing and Wharncliffe.

For a complete list of Pen and Sword titles please contact
Pen and Sword Books Limited
47 Church Street, Barnsley, South Yorkshire, S70 2AS, England
E-mail: enquiries@pen-and-sword.co.uk
Website: www.pen-and-sword.co.uk

Contents

Acknowledgements

Research for this book has taken place at a number of different archives. In particular, we would like to extend our thanks to Mark Stevens and the staff at Berkshire Record Office who gave helpful advice on Broadmoor records; and Mark Smith and Blair Bruce, archivists at Shetland Amenity Trust who assisted with the case of John Jameson. We thank the staff at the National Records of Scotland and the National Library of Scotland.

We would like to extend our grateful thanks to: Jane Draper, for her excellent proof reading skills; Susannah Burtinshaw, who patiently re-read many drafts and made valuable suggestions to improve the drama and suspense of several stories; Julia Capper, who provided a warm comfortable environment to work in and supplied delicious sandwiches, excellent cake and endless cups of tea; and Dr Keith Stewart of Stonehaven Heritage Society and his wife Lorraine for their assistance in researching details of 'the Urie Tragedy' and their wonderful hospitality on a very cold icy day.

Appreciative thanks are also extended to Laura Hirst, production manager at Pen & Sword and Jon Wilkinson, who has again designed a fantastic jacket cover for this book. Finally, we are indebted to Carol Trow for her assistance and expertise in editing *Madness, Murder and Mayhem*.

Introduction

On the evening of 15 May 1800, a farce called 'The Humourists' was performed at the Theatre Royal in Drury Lane, London. George III, together with his sons, the Prince of Wales and the Duke of York, attended the performance. As the king entered the royal box, James Hadfield, a former cavalry officer with an impressive military career, aimed his gun and pulled the trigger. His Majesty stopped and stood firmly while the would-be assassin was seized by members of the audience and taken into custody. Relieved that the king was safe, the National Anthem was sung with gusto before and after the play and every verse that referred to the safety of His Majesty received a thunder of applause.

This assassination attempt on the king changed the way in which criminals considered to be insane when committing their offence were dealt with by the criminal justice system. The perpetrator of the attempted murder, James Hadfield, was charged with both treason – which was a capital offence punishable by death – and attempted murder. However, Hadfield was acquitted on the grounds of 'insanity' – which at that time was defined as 'lost to all sense ... incapable of forming a judgement upon the consequences of the act which he is about to do'. Hadfield was not imprisoned, but was treated in an asylum for his mental health problems and remained there for the rest of his life.

The question of insanity had been widely discussed in government and medical circles due to the serendipitous circumstances surrounding the mania of the reigning monarch, George III. As a result, the beginning of the nineteenth century saw a change in perception and a more empathic approach to those suffering from mental illness. Although little understood and occasionally viewed as bizarre and freakish, it was also recognised that those considered to be insane were human beings and should be treated as such.

New legislation significantly altered the manner in which those with mental health disorders were treated. Manacles and chains which had previously been used to restrain 'lunatics' were discarded, and a caring approach to treatment was adopted. Squalid, dirty and prison-like conditions were abandoned and curative accommodation in hospital-like surroundings was provided. It was recognised that some mental health disorders could be alleviated by a humane approach to care. People with these types of problems began to be treated less like animals and more as individuals who had rights, hopes and a desire to be well.

Anthony Ashley-Cooper, Lord Ashley, who later became the 7th Earl of Shaftesbury, along with others of influence, recognised that the asylum system needed reform and together they helped enact profound and fundamental changes to benefit those with mental health disorders. He served on a Select Committee on Pauper Lunatics in the House of Commons and amendments were made to the lunacy laws to improve the admission, treatment and release of lunatics from asylums. These laws would also affect criminal lunatics, who as a result of the 1800 Criminal Lunatics Act and Treason Act, were detained indefinitely in a suitable asylum facility alongside non-criminal lunatics.

In many respects improved legislation also altered public perception about people who had previously been deemed 'abnormal'. The new asylums of the nineteenth century were considered to be curative shelters for people that society did not understand. They also became places where a new class of health professional – the 'mad doctor', 'alienist' or, as we term it today, 'psychiatrist' was trying to understand human mental affliction and finding ways to alleviate or cure it.

This book looks at changes to the treatment of the criminally insane during the Victorian and Edwardian periods. Beginning with three landmark cases which changed British legislation prior to the reign of Victoria, it endeavours to provide a flavour and description of some of the patients at Broadmoor Hospital – the purpose-built Criminal Lunatic Asylum for England and Wales and also the Criminal Lunatic Department at Perth Prison in Scotland. Chapters will look individually at those considered to be weak-minded, imbecile and idiot and also examines different forms of parricide as well as those who killed for gain. There was inevitably a great deal of evidence provided to courts to support people who claimed to be insane at the time of their offences. Many used this defence to avoid the noose. However, judge and jury did not always believe these claims even when supported by the most eminent of doctors. A chapter will show what happened to two individuals who were considered mentally irresponsible for their crimes by medical specialists in court but were hanged.

INTRODUCTION

Using case studies from England, Wales and Scotland, we will attempt to tell the stories of those who became patients at institutions for the criminally insane. Where possible, we will also follow the outcome of those left behind as a result of their crimes – the widows and orphans of not only the criminals but also their victims – to determine the impact criminal insanity had on their lives.

Chapter 1

Defining criminal insanity in the nineteenth century

During the first half of the nineteenth century three landmark cases ensured changes were made to legislation for those considered to be criminally insane. Although evolving over a 40-year period, these cases formed the backbone of 'new legislation' which remains in existence today – the M'Naughten Rules.

The first of the three incidents which required the government to take action was the attempted assassination of George III by former cavalry officer James Hadfield in 1800. This event, and the resulting court case, highlighted the inadequacies of contemporary law. It provided a major catalyst in establishing the 1800 Criminal Lunatics Act and the 1800 Treason Act both proposed by the prosecution four days after Hadfield's trial.

Prior to 1800, individuals who were acquitted of crimes by reason of insanity were set free and released into the safe-keeping of families or friends because there was no law under which they could be detained. This situation was radically altered after Hadfield's trial. The Criminal Lunatics Act ensured that those guilty of treason, murder, or felony, who were deemed to be insane would be detained indefinitely in a suitable asylum facility.

The terms of this Act, which received Royal Assent on 28 July 1800 included:

> 'If the jury shall find that such person was insane at the time of the committing such offence, the court before whom such trial shall be had, shall order such person to be kept in strict custody, in such place and in such manner as to the court shall seem fit, until His Majesty's pleasure shall be known.'

Many criminally insane prisoners were sent to Bethlehem Hospital in London, also known as Bethlem and colloquially referred to as 'Bedlam'.

State funding was obtained to build additional wards for the new category of 'criminal lunatic'. These were completed in 1816 following the asylum's move from Moorfields in 1815 to new premises in St George's Fields at Lambeth. At that time, it was not considered necessary to build a specific asylum for criminal lunatics. They were effectively allowed to enter any asylum where vulnerable insane patients were also housed. It would take another two murders before the legislation was further amended.

James Hadfield

James Hadfield (1771-1841) had served in the British Army as a cavalry officer with a record of heroic and exemplary conduct during the Anglo-Austrian campaign against the French in Flanders between 1793 and 1795. While acting as a captain in the 15th King's Regiment of Light Dragoons (Hussars) in May 1794, he was injured in combat and received multiple head injuries during the Battle of Tourcoing in the French Revolutionary Wars fought in northern France. Several blows from a sabre to the side of his head, followed by a cut to his left cheek, forced him off his horse and into a ditch on the battlefield. Presumed dead, he was found by two French officers who took him to a house containing the dead from the battle. The following day, he was discovered to still be alive and was provided with milk and water. Hadfield then walked to a British wagon and was transferred to a military hospital to receive treatment for his wounds.

Hadfield's experiences in battle and the trauma to his head and face left him in a very deranged state of mind and he began to suffer delusions of persecution, leading him to threaten to kill his own child. Hadfield was honourably discharged from the army in 1796 due to insanity. He never fully recovered from the ordeal of his war experiences. He became deluded, believing that in order to save the world and bring about the Second Coming of Jesus Christ, he must die at the hands of the British Government.

In order to guarantee this fate and hoping to be hanged, he devised a plan to shoot the king while he attended a play at the Theatre Royal on Drury Lane. Hadfield missed his target by over 14 inches and was tried for high treason. His barrister, Thomas Erskine, 1st Baron Erskine, argued that he was insane and suffering from delusions. Three medical men testified in court that the delusions were due to the severe head injuries sustained while on active military service for King and Country. The judge, Lloyd Kenyon, 1st Baron Kenyon, halted the trial declaring the verdict was clearly one of acquittal.

James Hadfield was admitted to Bethlehem Hospital and was one of the first patients to be detained in the new criminal lunatic wing when it opened in 1816. He remained there for the rest of his life, save for a short period in July 1802 when he escaped for four days. He died on 23 January 1841 at the age of 69 years from tuberculosis.

On the evening of 11 May 1812, another pivotal event took place which again highlighted the difficulties of assessing insanity in a court of law. The British prime minister, Spencer Perceval, was shot as he walked across the lobby of the House of Commons in the Palace of Westminster. The wound was fatal and Perceval fell face downwards. He was carried into the office of the Speaker's Secretary and placed on a table where he uttered a few convulsive sobs and died. A solicitor, Henry Burgess, and Lieutenant-General Isaac Gascoyne, Member of Parliament for Liverpool, were in the lobby at the time of the shooting and saw the man responsible for the murder – John Bellingham. He appeared to be sitting on a bench in great agitation. They approached him, took two loaded pistols and asked, 'what could have induced you to do such a thing'. Bellingham replied that 'he had been ill-used' and had a redress of grievance against the government. He was taken to Newgate Prison before appearing at the Old Bailey on a charge of murder.

John Bellingham

John Bellingham was born in St Neots, Huntingdonshire in 1769 but was brought up in London where he was apprenticed to a jeweller from the age of fourteen. He married Mary Neville in 1803 and the following year went to Arkhangelsk in Russia to work as an export representative for a London counting house. Imprisoned for a lengthy period by the Russian authorities due to supposed debt, Bellingham requested assistance from the British Ambassador, Lord Granville Leveson-Gower, which was not forthcoming. After his eventual release and return to England in 1809, he began a campaign to have his name cleared. Becoming increasingly frustrated at his lack of success, he determined to commit a crime that would ensure his name would not be forgotten – killing the prime minister.

Speaking eloquently at his trial at the Old Bailey, Bellingham gave a detailed account of the reasons for his grievance against the government. He blamed his lengthy incarceration in the Russian prison despite no wrongdoing on his part. He was particularly aggrieved at the lack of assistance from the British Ambassador.

Bellingham expressed regret at having killed a man against whom he had no personal grievance. Several witnesses spoke in his defence in an attempt to prove he was insane. The most compelling of these was a family friend, Ann Billett, who voluntarily travelled from Southampton to provide information about Bellingham's state of mind. She informed the court that his father had died in an asylum in Titchfield Street off Oxford Street in a state of insanity.

The Lord Chief Justice, Sir James Mansfield, summed up the evidence against Bellingham. In a show of great emotion including the shedding of tears, he described Spencer Perceval as 'a man so dear, and so revered'. The whole court was affected by Mansfield's words despite his reassurance that he did not wish to influence the jury by his personal emotion at the murder of such an 'excellent man'.

Speaking to the Old Bailey jury, Mansfield set out the evidence against Bellingham in terms of how insanity was perceived in law at that time:

> 'In another part of the prisoner's defence, which was not, however, urged by himself, it was attempted to be proved, that at the time of the commission of the crime he was insane. With respect to this the law was extremely clear, if a man was deprived of all power of reasoning, so as not to be able to distinguish whether it was right or wrong to commit the most wicked, or the most innocent transaction, he could not certainly commit an act against the law; such a man, so destitute of all power of judgment, could have no intention at all. In order to support this defence, it ought to be proved by the most distinct and unquestionable evidence, that the criminal was incapable of judging between right or wrong. There was no other proof of insanity which would excuse murder, or any other crime. There are various species of insanity. Some human creatures are void of all power of reasoning from their birth, such could not be guilty of any crime. There is another species of madness in which persons were subject to temporary paroxysms, in which they were guilty of acts of extravagance, this was called lunacy, if these persons committed a crime when they were not affected with the malady, they were to all intents and purposes amenable to justice: so long as they can

distinguish good from evil, so long are they answerable for their conduct. There is a third species of insanity, in which the patient fancied the existence of injury, and sought an opportunity of gratifying revenge, by some hostile act; if such a person was capable, in other respects, of distinguishing right from wrong, there is no excuse for any act of atrocity which he might commit under this description of derangement. The witnesses who had been called to support this extraordinary defence, had given a very singular account, to shew that at the, commission of the crime the prisoner was insane. What might have been the state of his mind some time ago, was perfectly immaterial. The single question is, whether at the time this fact was committed, he possessed a sufficient degree of understanding to distinguish good from evil, right from wrong, and whether murder was a crime not only against the law of God, but against the law of his country. Here it appears that the prisoner had gone out like another man; that he came up to London by himself, at Christmas last, that he was under no restraint, that no medical man had attended him to cure his malady, that he was perfectly regular in all his habits, in short there was no proof adduced to shew that his understanding was so deranged, as not to enable him to know that murder was a crime. On the contrary, the testimony adduced in his defence, has most distinctly proved, from a description of his general demeanour, that he was in every respect a full and competent judge of all his actions.'

Despite the evidence of family and friends to Bellingham's state of mind, Bellingham himself remained insistent throughout the trial that he was not insane.

The jury retired to consider their verdict. They returned after only 14 minutes to pronounce Bellingham guilty of murder. Bellingham was invited to comment on the verdict but was unable to utter any words. The Court Recorder addressed him as follows:

'Prisoner at the bar! You have been convicted by a most attentive and a most merciful jury, of one of the most malicious and atrocious crimes it is in the power of human nature to perpetrate – that of wilful and premeditated murder! A crime which in all ages and in all nations has been held in the deepest detestation – a crime as odious and abominable in the eyes of God, as it is hateful and abhorrent to the feelings of man. A crime which, although thus heinous in itself, in your case has been heightened by every possible feature of aggravation. You have shed the blood of a man admired for every virtue which can adorn public or private life – a man, whose suavity and meekness of manner was calculated to disarm all political rancour, and to deprive violence of its asperity. By his death, charity has lost one of its greatest promoters; religion, one of its firmest supporters; domestic society, one of its happiest and sweetest examples; and the country, one of its brightest ornaments – a man, whose ability and worth was likely to produce lasting advantages to this empire, and ultimate benefit to the world. Your crime has this additional feature of atrocious guilt, that in the midst of civil society, unarmed, defenceless, in the fulfilment of his public duty, and within the very verge of the sanctuary of the law, your impure hand has deprived of existence a man as universally beloved, as pre-eminent for his talents and excellence of heart.

'That you be taken from hence to the place from whence you came, and from thence to a place of execution, where you shall be hanged by the neck until you be dead; your body to be dissected and anatomized.'

Bellingham was hanged on 18 May 1812 – just one week after the murder of Spencer Perceval and before the defence witnesses had arrived from St Petersburg who would have provided firm evidence of his insanity. The Attorney-General, Sir Vicary Gibbs, hastily refused to postpone the hearing of the case. The night before his execution, Bellingham wrote a last letter to his wife.

'My Blessed Mary,
It rejoiced me beyond measure to hear you are likely to be provided for. I am sure the public at large will participate and mitigate your sorrows. I assure you, my love, my sincerest endeavours have ever been directed to your welfare. As we shall not meet any more in this world, I sincerely hope we shall do so in the world to come.

My blessing to the boys, with kind remembrance to Miss Stevens, for whom I have the greatest regard, in consequence of her uniform affection for them. With the purest of intentions it has always been my misfortune to be thwarted, misrepresented, and ill-used in life but, however, we feel a happy prospect of compensation in a speedy translation to life eternal. It's not possible to be more calm or placid that I feel; and nine hours more will waft me to those happy shores where bliss is without alloy.
Yours ever affectionate,
John Bellingham
Sunday night, 11 o'clock.

'Dr Ford will forward you my watch, prayer book with a guinea and note. Once more, God be with you my sweet Mary. The public sympathises much for me, but I have been called upon to play an anxious card in life.'

Bellingham remained composed to the end. He stated categorically before his execution that he 'bore no resentment to Mr Perceval as a man and as a man I am sorry for his fate. It was my own sufferings that caused the melancholy event'. He asked that the Perceval family should be informed that he had a deep contrition for his actions.

Public sympathy for Bellingham was high. It was believed that he had suffered a miscarriage of justice. The Attorney-General was criticised for his conduct of the case and for his refusal to postpone his judgement before the evidence of the Russian witnesses could be heard. Bellingham's wife and their three sons found themselves destitute and a public subscription was opened for them by the people of Liverpool where Mary had a millinery business. Lord Granville Leveson-Gower, the former ambassador to Russia whom Bellingham blamed for his misfortunes, donated £50 to the fund. In order to distance herself and her sons from the public eye, Mary reverted to her maiden surname of Neville. Her three sons: James born in 1801 in Russia; William born in 1806 in Lancashire; and Henry Stevens born in 1811 in Liverpool also took the Neville surname. Mary Neville married James Raymond Barker in 1813 and the couple settled in Highbury Grove, London where she died in 1853.

Spencer Perceval's widow, Jane Perceval née Wilson, was granted an annuity of £2,000 and her twelve surviving children £50,000 by both

Houses of Parliament shortly after her husband's assassination. Perceval was buried in the family vault in Charlton, Kent. A large cortège followed the hearse from Downing Street to its final resting place and the coffin bore the inscription:

Right Honorable SPENCER PERCEVAL
Chancellor of the Exchequer, First Lord of the Treasury,
Prime Minister of England,
Fell by the Hand of an ASSASSIN in the Commons
House of Parliament, May 11, A.D. 1812, in the 50th
year of his age; born, Nov. 1st, A.D. 1762

Spencer Perceval was the son of John Perceval, 2nd Earl of Egmont, a renowned genealogist of his day who also served as First Lord of the Admiralty, and his wife Catherine Compton. Following his death, his widow married Lieutenant-Colonel Sir Henry Carr. She died in 1844. The couple's eldest son, Spencer, served as a Metropolitan Lunacy Commissioner while a younger son John Thomas Perceval spent three years in a lunatic asylum in the 1830s. Placed there by his family, John spent the rest of his life highlighting the poor treatment he had received and in 1838 published a book entitled *A narrative of the treatment experienced by a Gentleman during a state of mental derangement designed to explain the causes and nature of insanity, and to expose the injudicious conduct pursued towards many unfortunate sufferers under that calamity.*

Had John Bellingham pleaded insanity at his trial, without doubt, he would not have been hanged and would have spent the rest of his life in a lunatic asylum.

There were several attempts on the life of Queen Victoria at the beginning of her reign, such as that of Edward Oxford who fired a pistol at her in London in June 1840. Another pivotal assassination attempt took place in 1843 which outraged the public. It was very similar to the Bellingham case.

Daniel M'Naughten

On 20 January 1843, Daniel M'Naughten (1813-65), a wood-turning lathe worker from Glasgow, was determined to kill the British prime minister, Sir Robert Peel. M'Naughten was possessed by paranoid delusions that government spies were following him. He believed that the only way they could be stopped was by killing the prime minister. Fortunately for Peel, M'Naughten mistook his private secretary, Edward Drummond, for him and it was Drummond who was shot in the back. The incident was witnessed by Police Constable James Silver who after a significant struggle wrestled two firearms from M'Naughten and arrested him. He was taken to Bow Street Police Station where he asserted that:

> 'The Tories in my native city have driven me to this, and have followed me to France, Scotland, and other parts; I can get no sleep from the system they pursue towards me; I believe I am driven into a consumption by them; they wish to murder me. That is all I wish to say at present; they have completely disordered me, and I am quite a different man before they commenced this annoyance towards me.'

Edward Drummond was taken the short distance from Whitehall to a private room at his brother's banking house in Charing Cross Road. He was attended by Richard Jackson, surgeon and apothecary. From there he was taken to his own home at 19, Grosvenor Street where the bullet was removed. Initially his condition was considered to be stable. It was believed that he would recover. However, after five days, with his sister by his side, he passed away. He was aware that his life was coming to an end and stated:

> 'I have endeavoured to live honestly doing as much good as I could, and I place my hope in God's mercy for my redemption. I don't feel any pain, that ugly French word malaise expresses most fully my burden.'

Daniel M'Naughten underwent a lengthy trial at the Old Bailey. His father, also named Daniel M'Naughten, many of his acquaintances and leading medical experts were questioned about his state of mind. M'Naughten was acquitted – absolved of liability as insane and consequently not accountable for his actions. The verdict outraged the public and ensured that insanity was redefined in criminal law.

The subsequent House of Lords review determined that the law had to prove whether the defendant knew what he was doing at the time of the crime and, if so, that he was aware that it was wrong. Following this ruling, individuals deemed to be insane were treated differently within the judicial system. This test for criminal insanity became known as the 'M'Naughten Rules' and remains in force in the United Kingdom today.

Daniel M'Naughten spent the rest of his life in an asylum, predominantly Bethlehem, but he was transferred to Broadmoor when the male wards opened in 1864 and died there the following year of heart and kidney disease.

In a cruel twist of fate, the murders of Spencer Perceval and Edward Drummond were connected by more than their positions of authority and the grievances of their assassins against the government. Spencer Perceval's sister, Mary, married Andrew Berkeley Drummond, brother of Edward's father, Robert, on 2 April 1781. Thus, Mary Perceval became Edward Drummond's aunt by marriage. The two men are buried in the same family tomb in Charlton, Kent.

Chapter 2

Specialist provision for the criminally insane

In Britain, from 1843, criminals deemed to be insane were treated differently by the judiciary following the trial of Daniel M'Naughten. However, at this stage in England and Wales there was no established method to house criminal patients separately within the asylum system where the majority were 'detained at Her Majesty's pleasure'.

Lord Shaftesbury motioned the House of Commons in 1852 to build a separate facility for criminal lunatics in England and Wales. He produced reams of testimony from medical superintendents from several asylums to prove that permitting criminals to be housed alongside vulnerable insane patients was detrimental. He approved of the new facility built at Dundrum for the criminally insane in Ireland. Lord Shaftesbury's list of principal reasons assigned by the superintendents of asylums for the non-association of criminal lunatics with ordinary lunatic patients stated:

'It is unjust to ordinary patients to associate them with persons branded with crime. The lunatic is generally very sensitive, and both he and his friends feel aggrieved and degraded by the association. The moral effect is bad. The conduct of criminal patients is frequently very violent; their habits and language, the result of previous habits, are frequently offensive, and their influence on other patients injurious and pernicious. By the fact of stricter custody being required, and greater responsibility felt for criminal patients, the general classification of patients in an asylum is interrupted, and the improved discipline and proper treatment of other patients interfered with; the expense is also increased for safe keeping. The common delusion that an asylum is a prison is strengthened by lunatic patients being compelled to associate with persons who have been in prison; and, in fact, higher walls than those ordinarily in use have been considered necessary (and in one case erected) for the security of criminal lunatics associated with other patients. The association is injurious even to the criminal patients. It exposes them to taunts from the other patients, and the stricter confinement imposed on themselves irritates them. They are irritated also when other patients are liberated, and they left in confinement. When criminal patients are confided in (in the same way as other patients), it is generally found that they are unworthy of trust; that they try to escape and induce others to do so, and that insubordination and dissatisfaction are generally produced by their influence. The criminal patients concentrate attention on themselves, and attract an undue share of care and supervision from the attendants. Cases of simulated insanity are (supposed to be) not infrequent with patients received as criminal lunatics. In those cases the patients are mostly patients of the worst character. They create discontent among the other patients, and oppress those who are weaker than themselves, and they generally try to escape. Patients of the criminal class, even when unsound at the time of committing the offence, possess criminal propensities, and in some cases their insanity has been caused by vicious habits. The most efficient remedy for this state of things, would, in my opinion, be the establishment of a State asylum for the separate care and custody of those who were termed criminal lunatics; and for this I have the approbation of almost all the medical superintendents and persons most conversant with lunacy throughout the United Kingdom.'

Sir William Charles Hood graduated as a Doctor of Medicine at the University of St Andrews in 1846. As an experienced medical superintendent, he was appointed to Bethlehem Hospital as its first ever Resident Physician-Superintendent in 1852 – a post he held until 1862. Hood was instrumental in reforming the medical administration of Bethlehem, separating criminal lunatics from others who were insane and he promoted non-restraint and other compassionate advances until his death in 1870.

Previously, Bethlehem was seen by many as a charitable madhouse that housed idiots and imbeciles. Under Hood, Bethlehem's reputation developed to reflect the transformation from a punitive prison to a hospital caring for people with mental illnesses. Consequently, the public's view of Bethlehem changed positively throughout Hood's superintendence. From the time of his appointment he was in control of the asylum with 'paramount authority' – a move required by the Lunacy Commission who wanted doctors rather than administrators to run asylums. After his resignation from Bethlehem in 1862, William Charles Hood became a Lord Chancellor's Visitor in Lunacy and was knighted in 1868.

Following the Criminal Lunatics Act of 1800, more people were sent from the courts to be detained until 'His/Her Majesty's pleasure be known' on the ground of insanity. The most dangerous were sent to Bethlehem but others found their way to Fisherton House, which had been established in 1813 as a private 'madhouse' in the village of Fisherton Anger, west of Salisbury, Wiltshire. The house in Wilton Road was purchased by Charles Finch at the start of the nineteenth century. From 1813, when the first patient was admitted, until 1954, when it was absorbed into the NHS as the Old Manor Hospital, it was essentially a private lunatic asylum, owned and managed by members of the same family – the Finches. In its day, it was the largest private madhouse in England. The hospital finally closed in 2003.

The asylum was initially run by Charles' nephew, Dr William Corbin Finch, a London surgeon, who also oversaw three other private madhouses at Laverstock House near Salisbury, Kensington House in Kensington, London and The Retreat in Kings Road, Chelsea, London. Fisherton accepted both private and pauper patients. By 1837 it housed 100 patients – of whom 60 were paupers.

In 1848, the proprietors, in an arrangement with the Government, built new wards to house the overflow from Bethlehem – mainly the less dangerous criminal lunatics. By 1853, Fisherton housed 214 patients cared for by 26 attendants. Like Bethlehem, Fisherton House soon filled to capacity and in 1856 the Government examined the need to build a specialist asylum.

Determining that such a facility was required, the concept of Broadmoor Hospital for the Criminally Insane was born. The Criminal Lunatic Asylums Act of 1860 (known colloquially as the Broadmoor Act) allowed the government to build a specialist facility. Those deemed to be dangerous should be kept away from those considered likely of a cure.

Broadmoor was built near the village of Crowthorne, Berkshire between 1856 and 1863, designed by Sir Joshua Jebb, a military engineer who had previously planned two prisons – Pentonville in London and Mountjoy in Dublin. It was constructed using labour provided by convicts from the Isle of Wight. In keeping with asylum guidelines, it was situated in attractive countryside with a large and spacious building close to a railway station to facilitate the movement of patients.

The first patients transferred from Bethlehem on 27 May 1863 were eight women. Of these, six had killed or wounded their children using a variety of different methods. A further 90 women were admitted that year. Broadmoor opened its doors to 221 male patients on 27 February 1864. Numbers fluctuated slightly but there were generally about 500 patients in the asylum at any one time in the 1870s.

There were two classes of patient – Queen's or King's pleasure patients who had been found to be insane at the time of their trials, and prisoners previously housed in other correctional institutions who became insane during their incarceration. Both classes of patient could eventually be released or transferred following appropriate treatment. Individuals were treated as patients rather than criminals and came from all over England and Wales and from all social classes. Visitors were rare due to the huge distances involved in travelling to Berkshire.

Despite this facility, not all criminal lunatics were admitted to Broadmoor. Many individuals guilty of less serious crimes and with shorter sentences were maintained either in a local prison or transferred to a district asylum.

In Scotland, the Prisons (Scotland) Act of 1844 defined criminal lunatics as 'insane persons charged with serious offences'. As would later occur in England, the main instigators for specialist provision for the criminally insane were medical superintendents who objected to 'the insane being associated with persons who had been charged with committing violent and heinous crimes'. It was believed that a prison asylum which could ensure the close and safe custody of the most dangerous class of lunatics was needed.

From 1846, criminal lunatics in Scotland were housed in a special department in the General Prison at Perth. This bleak and unwelcoming building had originally been used to detain French prisoners-of-war during the Napoleonic campaigns at the beginning of the nineteenth century. It was converted into a 'Criminal Lunatic Department' on two floors, initially with accommodation for 35 males and 13 females. The men and women were separated by strong partition walls. The first inmate was a mischievous 11-year-old boy, John Jameson, admitted in December 1846 (see Chapter 4).

The Scottish Lunacy Commission visited in May 1855 when there were twenty-one male and six female patients. They reported:

'The whole of the lower storey, and half of the upper one, is occupied by the men; the women are placed in the remaining half of the upper floor. The accommodation on the ground-floor consists of a series of cells, each containing from one to four beds; and of two day rooms, placed in single range along the galleries. The cells are generally very gloomy, and are mostly flagged. The windows are strongly barred, placed high in the wall, beyond the reach of the patients. The doors are of great strength. Cells in the cross galleries are warmed by heated air, but those in the central gallery have no means of receiving heat. The two day rooms contain tables and benches without backs and have open fire-places with strong iron gratings. The accommodation on the female side consists of a day-room, and several cells with one, two, or three beds in each.

'There are lavatories in the galleries, and a warm bath on each side, which is used by the patients once a month. There are two airing courts for the males enclosed by high walls, and one for the females which is more cheerful than the others, possessing a limited view of the surrounding country.

There are four male and one female attendants. The whole arrangements are made principally with a view to the security of the patients, and scarcely, if at all, with their treatment as sufferers from disease. The male patients are without the means of occupation or recreation. Some of the females do a little sewing. Both sexes spend a great part of the day in the airing-yards in a state of listlessness. Two patients are habitually under restraint.'

The conditions found at Perth were inferior to those contained within the newly built asylum for English and Welsh patients. In 1882, Matthew Jackson Hunter, a 27-year-old clerk, found guilty of murdering his wife and child earlier the same year wrote to his sister detailing his pleasant surroundings at Broadmoor:

'It is a splendid block of buildings ... pleasantly situated, has an extensive view and is very healthy. We have three doctors who visit us every day, and the patients spend most of their time exercising in the gardens, reading the daily papers, monthly periodicals, etc. There is also a well selected library, a cricket club, billiards, cards, and other amusements. In the wintertime we have entertainments given by the patients, such as plays, singing, etc. We have a good brass band. We have good food, plenty of clean clothes, good beds and bedding, and every comfort that one need expect are treated with kindness by the officials placed over us, and have free conversation among other patients.'

In Scotland conditions in the middle of the nineteenth century were far from ideal as indicated in the Commissioners' Report above. All the changes throughout Britain were considered by many asylum medical superintendents as beneficial, proving that the disassociation of criminal and 'ordinary' lunatics was a positive step forward.

Criminal lunatic asylums were constructed not only to treat the insane but also to protect non-criminal lunatics, the general public and asylum staff. However, as will be seen in chapter 5 this was not always successful.

Chapter 3

The first female patients

The Criminal Lunatic Department of the General Prison at Perth received its first female patient, Mary Paterson, in 1847. Convicted of fire raising in 1842, and originally held at the Royal Asylum of Edinburgh, she was transferred to the new unit at Perth and remained there for nearly 30 years, categorised as an imbecile. Details of her case are given in Chapter 6. Very few women were incarcerated but another fascinating case where a woman was held until she died is that of Rebecca Bergenstein.

Rebecca Mason

Rebecca Bergenstein was born in Stanislauff, Poland in about 1820, a Jewess of eastern European extraction. She became the second wife of Dr John Mason, born in 1808 in Wigtown, Wigtownshire. Dr Mason, accompanied by his first wife and their son, John McGeorge Mason, born in Antigua about 1833, was physician and surgeon to the garrison on the Swedish island of St Bartholomew in the West Indies from 1836 to 1842. A daughter, Mary Euphemia, was born on St Bartholomew in 1837. In 1846, Dr Mason, now a widower, officiated as a medical missionary from the Free Church of Scotland to the Jews in Turkey. He met 28-year-old Rebecca Bergenstein there and, influencing her away from Judaism and towards Christianity, they married in Constantinople in 1849. John and Rebecca returned to the south of Scotland later that year and re-married at Dumfries on 12 November 1849. Rebecca gave up her Jewish faith and converted to the Free Church of Scotland. She was baptised at Rev William Clark's church at Maxwelltown, Dumfries on 18 November 1849 before a vast crowd. The newly married couple together with the children from John's first marriage moved to a house in the Main Street of Gatehouse-of-Fleet, Kirkcudbrightshire, 30 miles from Dumfries.

Marital bliss did not last long. On 17 August 1850, as John was having his morning wash, Rebecca pierced him in the throat with his razor. She continued to stab him in the neck, head, legs, arms and various other parts of his body. But she did not kill him.

Rebecca was charged with stabbing and cutting her 41-year-old husband with the intention of murdering him. She alleged that John had behaved cruelly and harshly towards her and had driven her to desperation and insanity – providing an element of provocation in her attack. Evidence proved that there were frequent disputes between the couple. Rebecca was suffering from insomnia, anorexia and an insensibility to cold. She did not take meals regularly and she imagined that her husband was putting poison in her tea in order to kill her.

Her trial took place at the High Court in Edinburgh on 12 March 1851. Rebecca was represented by Alexander Logan, advocate, who entered a plea of insanity. She was found insane, suffering from a religious monomania. The Court found that her mind was deeply possessed with the idea that she had an assurance of salvation and she believed that everyone else was a child of the Devil who tormented her. She was unanimously found unfit for trial and was ordered to be confined in the prison of Edinburgh subject to further orders of the Court.

Rebecca was transferred from Edinburgh Prison to Perth on 14 March 1851 where she died 47 years later on 24 April 1898. An inquiry into her death revealed that she had died of natural causes due to senile decay.

John Mason began a new life without his wife and in the early 1850s moved to Northumberland where he continued to work as a medical practitioner. He made his home with a recently widowed lady, Mary Young, and her four young children. The 1861 census shows that John and Mary claimed to be married and had a son called John McGeorge Mason, born in 1857. This was the same name as his eldest son by his first wife who died aged 20 years in October 1853 in Morpeth, Northumberland.

When Broadmoor Hospital opened in 1863, female patients deemed to be criminally insane were transferred from various district asylums to Bethlehem. From there, they were removed in groups of about eight patients at a time every three or four days to Broadmoor. The accommodation on the female side of the hospital was completed nine months before the more extensive male quarters. Therefore, the first patients to be transferred from Bethlehem in May 1863 were women. By the end of the month, 17 had been admitted. Transfers continued throughout the year from other establishments and by the end of 1863, 95 female patients had been moved to Broadmoor. Of these, many were women who had killed or wounded their children.

Martha Bacon

Martha Bacon, was born in Marston Trussell, Northamptonshire in 1830, the daughter of George and Sarah Judkins. She married Thomas Fuller Bacon on 10 September 1850 in Chelsea. The following year the couple were living in Stamford, Lincolnshire where Thomas was employed as a whitesmith. By 1856, they had two children – a son, Edwin Fuller in 1854, and a daughter, Sarah Ann in 1856. Following the birth of Sarah Ann, Martha began to suffer from acute mania and delusions. On 13 June 1856, she was admitted to St Luke's Asylum, London. After four months, she returned home and was seen to treat her children with great fondness. Just six months later, Edwin and Sarah Ann were found dead. Martha had slit their throats and then attempted to cut her own.

Martha was charged at the Police Court in Lambeth with murdering her children on 29 December 1856. Described in one newspaper as 'a respectable married woman', Martha stated that she was innocent of the crime; insisting that a man had climbed in through a window the previous evening, murdered her children, and then tried to murder her.

Although Martha remained in police custody, there was some doubt as to whether she had actually committed the crime. Martha's husband, Thomas, was suspected of being the actual murderer, and of using his wife's previous bout of insanity as a convenient means of declaring himself innocent. Blood was found on items of his clothing and Martha claimed that her husband had tried to strangle her with a piece of rope which was later found at their home. The Matron of Horsemonger Lane Gaol gave evidence that Martha had a mark around her neck as if she had been strangled and also a wound on her throat made by a knife. While in gaol, Martha wrote a letter stating:

> 'Sir, I must confess that I am an innocent person, and he who committed the dreadful deed is my husband, and there was no money in the drawers. He took the little boy downstairs, put him in a chair, and there cut his throat; he then went upstairs, and cut the little baby's throat. Signed, Martha Bacon.'

Both Martha and Thomas Bacon stood trial in April 1857 at the Old Bailey for the murders of their children. Despite a great deal of speculation regarding the likelihood that Thomas Bacon had murdered his children, the jury found him not guilty and blamed Martha for the crime. However, she was found not guilty due to insanity and was ordered to be detained at Her Majesty's pleasure.

As there was no dedicated criminal lunatic asylum in England at that time, Martha was admitted to Bethlehem. She was described as having a 'moderate' degree of education and her countenance was one of 'mildness and good nature' and her conduct was marked by 'kindness, amiability and industry'. Her crime was considered atrocious, made worse by the fact that she had tried to implicate her husband in the offence. Interestingly, the Bethlehem case notes reveal that Thomas Bacon:

> 'was subsequently convicted of the murder of his mother whose death occurred some months before under suspicious circumstances. The body was exhumed and poison discovered.'

Following his trial with Martha for the murder of their children, Thomas was taken to Stamford Gaol and was tried for the murder of his mother, Ann, who had died on 15 May 1855. On 6 February 1857, Ann Bacon's body was exhumed from Great Casterton Churchyard in Rutland. A post mortem examination discovered such a large amount of arsenic in her body that many of her vital organs had been well preserved despite her having died nearly two years previously. Thomas Fuller Bacon was tried at Lincoln Assizes on 25 July 1857 before Mr Justice (Sir William) Erle. The main case for the prosecution was that Thomas, believing himself likely to inherit several properties on his mother's death, had purchased arsenic and administered it to her to hasten her demise. He was found guilty of her murder and the judge passed the death sentence.

Thomas Bacon was saved from the noose and, in 1862, was transported to Western Australia aboard the *Merchantman* with 192 other convicts. He died on 16 July 1869 at the prison hospital in Fremantle of renal disease. Martha, was not reprieved as a result of the verdict on her husband and was among the first patients transferred to Broadmoor on 30 May 1863.

She requested her release in 1870 and her brother, William Judkins, was contacted to ask whether he would provide her with a home. Unfortunately, he replied that her family were not willing to have her back and she was effectively cut off from her relatives. Martha did receive support from her brother-in-law and his wife, John and Mary Ann Bacon. John Bacon was her husband's elder brother and lived in Dover where he had a watch and clock making business. John wrote regularly to Broadmoor to enquire after Martha's health and Mary Ann sent her food-parcels. Martha remained in Broadmoor until her death from cancer of the stomach in 1899.

Ann Coultass

Thirty-four-year old Ann Coultass and her illegitimate son Willy lived with her brothers who were glass makers in Eccleston, St Helens, Lancashire. Ann acted as their housekeeper and there were also three lodgers in the same house – William Ewing with his wife and mother-in-law. Ann Coultass was considered to be a 'kind-hearted, creditable and steady creature' but following the death of her mother in 1857, she began to drink incessantly. Her dependence on alcohol made her despondent and irritable and she became melancholic and suicidal. She started to carry a razor and on several occasions threatened to hurt her child.

The lodgers were concerned for the safety of young Willy when his mother was drunk and often took him into their portion of the house until she sobered up. At about five o'clock on 22 August 1858 Ann Coultass collected her son from the care of the lodgers – it was to be the last time Willy was seen alive.

The following morning, Ann took a floor-brush and hot water to her room and spent a considerable amount of time cleaning. When asked about the whereabouts of Willy she replied that he had had two bad epileptic fits in the night and was asleep in bed. Her friend Mrs Hudspeth arrived at the house and, alarmed at Ann's manner, asked to see Willy. Both Mrs Hudspeth and Mrs Ewing accompanied her to her room, where they found Willy lying in bed with a linen bandage around his throat. Removing the bandage, they discovered something horrific – a deep wound across Willy's throat which had severed the jugular vein. Flinging herself across her son's body, Ann wept 'Oh my God what have I done?'.

She was arrested for his murder and taken into custody. She was tried at Liverpool Assizes on 16 December 1858. Her defence council, Dr Wheeler, addressed the jury on Ann's behalf and contended that her melancholy mania justified a verdict of not guilty on the ground of insanity. All but one member of the jury agreed and Ann was removed to Kirkdale Gaol.

She was transferred to Bethlehem on 9 April 1861 despite having shown no sign of insanity while in Kirkdale. Although somewhat melancholic, the medical staff at Bethlehem also found that she showed no signs of active insanity and was well behaved and industrious. Ann was one of the first group of patients to be transferred to Broadmoor on 27 May 1863. She died there from fatty degeneration of the heart on 28 April 1884.

Mary Ann Ogden

Mary Ann Saunders was born in Boxmoor, Hertfordshire in 1816. She had suffered from bouts of insanity as a teenager which necessitated her admission to Peckham House Asylum in Camberwell, Surrey. Recovering from her mental health problems, she married John Henry Ogden, who was a porter at Guy's Hospital, on 7 August 1842. In 1849, the couple were living at 14, Guy Street, Snowsfields in Bermondsey, London.

Mary Ann's husband was a violent, dissipated and controlling man who was convinced that his wife was unfaithful. Despite there being no evidence to suggest her infidelity and attempting to catch her with other men, he took to coming home late at night hoping to find her in a compromising situation. The couple remained childless for seven years before Mary Ann gave birth to a daughter, also named Mary Ann. Certain that the baby girl was not his, her husband became more violent towards her. Only a month after giving birth, Mary Ann drowned her daughter in a copper bath.

Unable to account for her actions and clearly very depressed, she was arrested and taken to Horsemonger Lane Gaol. A coroner's enquiry was held at the Britannia Inn on Nelson Street, Snowsfields and the jury declared a verdict of 'wilful murder'. She was due to be tried at the Old Bailey before Sir William Henry Maule. However, it became obvious that she was unwell and Mr Gilbert McMurdo, the surgeon of the gaol, gave evidence that she was not in a fit state of mind to plead. Mary Ann was detained at Her Majesty's pleasure and sent to Bethlehem on 6 April 1850 where she was diagnosed with puerperal insanity following recent childbirth. Her case notes reveal that her mother was a patient in Bedford Asylum and that her husband, John, drowned himself in Regent's Canal in London in 1853.

Mary Ann died in Broadmoor on 23 February 1890 of old age and general decay and is buried in the Church of St John the Baptist, Crowthorne.

Mary Chinn

Mary Chinn was the daughter of Thomas and Sarah Chinn. In 1852, although 26 years of age, she still lived in the family home in Coles Yard, Long Street, Atherstone, Warwickshire. She had been unable to work as a domestic servant for some time due to bouts of depression. Living in the same Yard, were the Barnes family comprising of George, a bricklayer's labourer, his wife Mary, and their four children: Joseph; David; Sarah; and two-year-old William.

On 9 August 1852, Mary Chinn, entered her neighbour's house and spoke to the Barnes' eldest son Joseph, who was about 10 years old. Mary was a frequent visitor to the Barnes home and was very fond of young William whom she cared for on a regular basis. Joseph was holding him in his arms when Mary arrived and taking the child from him, she asked him to go and fetch her mother.

When Mary's mother arrived at the house with Joseph they discovered that the door had been locked. Sarah Chinn lifted Joseph through an open window and he saw Mary standing by a tub of water with the legs of his small brother, William, sticking out from it. The alarm was raised and medical assistance sought to resuscitate William but to no affect. Mary appeared quite pleased with what she had done. She said that 'she wished to die; that she should have to repent, and should go to Heaven; and that the child not having committed any sin would certainly go to Heaven'.

Mary was in a very wild and excited state and the doctor was of the opinion that she was not aware that she had done anything wrong. At the ensuing coroner's inquest, she was asked to account for her actions. She willingly stated that she had killed William Barnes on purpose. To a further query regarding her mental state she commented, 'I have been in my senses all my lifetime'.

Mary was sent to Warwick County Lunatic Asylum. The medical superintendent, Dr William Henry Parsey, provided evidence at her trial in Coventry that she was insane. It was explained that, after the age of 18 years, Mary began to complain of delusions. She feared that her clothes were covered with worms which needed to be shaken off. She informed Dr Parsey that her head was being drawn by the ends of her nerves and that she felt everything she did would injure some insect or dumb animal.

Mary was convicted of wilful murder, and detained at Her Majesty's pleasure, initially in Warwick Gaol but then transferred to Bethlehem on 26 April 1855. On 10 September 1858, she was moved to Fisherton House

Asylum in Wiltshire. Her admission record and case notes from Bethlehem show that she was melancholic. The medical officers who examined her thought that the primary cause of her depression was over-studying the Bible. It was decided that she was showing signs of imbecility as she behaved in a childlike manner and said foolish things.

Mary was concerned that she had caused injury to someone without knowing it and took great care of the flies on the ward in case she harmed them. She was moved to Broadmoor on 5 June 1863 and died there on 19 April 1876 from dropsy and heart disease. She is buried in the churchyard of St John the Baptist in Crowthorne.

Hannah Smith

The eldest of the first group of female patients to be admitted to Broadmoor was 68-year-old Hannah Smith. Hannah had been convicted of wilful murder at Stafford Lent Assizes in 1837 and held at His Majesty's pleasure at Bethlehem as she was deemed to be of unsound mind.

Hannah and her husband, Thomas, lived in Darlaston, Staffordshire with their seven children. They were respectable people of middling fortune but tragedy struck the family in 1835 when Thomas committed suicide by drowning in a well. Hannah struggled to cope without him, attempted suicide and began to neglect herself and her family. She spent days at a time lying in bed and had to be prompted to get up and wash herself. She and her children moved to the home of her sister and brother-in-law, George Wilkes who was a gun-lock filer in Darlaston.

On Saturday 4 February 1837, Hannah and her youngest child, Samuel, aged six, were in the kitchen helping with the early morning chores while George Wilkes was packing locks into a basket. Shortly after, he heard the boy cry out from the yard opposite the house. Running outside, he saw Hannah holding Samuel by the neck and thighs as she attempted to drop him into the well. Samuel was crying and George rushed forward to prevent him from being dropped – but he was too late and he heard Samuel splash into the water. Pushing Hannah out of the way, and with the assistance of a rope and a man from the village, they attempted to save the boy. Unfortunately, it was more than half an hour before the body could be retrieved. Mr Rooker, the local surgeon, arrived immediately and attempted to revive him by putting him in a hot bath and rubbing his body with salt to restore animation but all attempts to resuscitate him were unsuccessful.

Following her conviction at Stafford Assizes on 15 March 1837, where she was described as having an insatiable venereal appetite and a persistent refusal to eat in order to kill herself, she was sent to Bethlehem. She remained there for the next 26 years. When Hannah arrived there, it was noted that her intellect had been impaired following the death of her husband that left her and her children destitute. Further impairment occurred when a gypsy warned her that she would destroy her children.

By 20 August 1846, she was deemed to be sane in the Bethlehem quarterly returns to the Lunacy Commissioners and her family and friends requested that she be released. Her brother, Francis Taylor of Darlaston, applied to the Home Secretary for her return to her family. He, and other relations, were caring for Hannah's children and they wished her to be reunited with them. Unfortunately, before a decision could be made, the medical attendants at Bethlehem reported a relapse in Hannah's mental health and she was not allowed to return to her family.

By 1854, Hannah had become a quiet, inoffensive and retiring woman who rarely left her bedroom. She seldom spoke and was very despondent suffering from frequent febrile attacks which lasted two to three days. It was thought that the main cause of her despondency at this stage in her life was the death of her only daughter Elizabeth who, finding herself pregnant and unmarried, had taken medicine to cause an abortion which resulted in her loss of life.

Hannah died in Broadmoor on 3 January 1871 of paralysis and old age.

Isabella Falcon

Isabella Falcon had also been in Bethlehem for many years when Broadmoor opened. She had been convicted of the gruesome murder of an elderly pauper inmate at Ellenborough Workhouse near Maryport in Cumberland in 1839.

Isabella was born about 1813, the daughter of Joseph Falcon, a clogger, and his wife Jane. Isabella had spent time in an asylum suffering from monomania following the death of a child, but in her mid-twenties was transferred to Ellenborough Workhouse. Considered to be recovered from her mania, she was allowed to work in the workhouse kitchen with other inmates. While she sat peeling potatoes with an elderly inmate called Jane Ray, believed to be 95 years old, Isabella, without apparent provocation, attacked Jane using the knife she was holding. The assault was so ferocious that despite the speedy arrival of the workhouse surgeon, Mr Gregg, Jane Ray was all but decapitated.

Isabella was tried in Carlisle in February 1839. Found to be insane at the time the murder was committed, she was detained at Her Majesty's pleasure. She was initially admitted to Gateshead Asylum but was transferred to Bethlehem on 20 June 1860. The medical staff considered her to be a weak, feeble and demented imbecile.

The staff at Bethlehem had great difficulty understanding her speech because of her strong northern dialect. She appeared scared and shrank away from all contact when she was first admitted and it was believed that she had been poorly treated in Gateshead. Treatment with kindness proved a positive influence and she gradually began to trust the staff. As a result, she took more notice of her appearance and also happily engaged in needlework.

In 1861 it was noted that for about ten days every month she descended into complete dementia and lost her appetite. At other times she was greedy and miserly and begged anyone who entered the ward for a halfpenny. This resulted in her accumulating a large number of coins some of which she secreted in her vagina. A decision was made to transfer her to Broadmoor. She was admitted on 30 May 1863 and remained there for the rest of her life, dying on 15 April 1881 of atrophic softening of the brain and old age. After her death, attempts were made to determine her next of kin so that they could be informed and Richard Falcon, an Innkeeper from Ellenborough, the illegitimate son of Isabella's sister was traced and contacted. There is no suggestion that Isabella ever received any communication from her family following her incarceration but her nephew, Richard, had a daughter in 1868 whom he named after his aunt.

Sarah Allen

Sarah Harris was born in Tintern Abbey, Monmouthshire, Wales in 1823, the daughter of William Harris, a farmer, and his wife Elizabeth Reece. In Swansea on 30 March 1848, Sarah married William Allen from Little Bardfield, Essex. The couple moved to London, setting up home in Chelsea. William was employed as a messenger at a steam-boat company. Their first child, William George, was born in 1849 and, by 1855, the couple had three sons with Edward John born in 1852 and Arthur Joshua in 1855. Sarah became unwell following the birth of her youngest child and she spent time recuperating in Hastings and then Essex before moving home to 2, Poulton Terrace, Chelsea.

The family appeared to have a happy home. Sarah was a kind and affectionate wife and mother. William was a sober, respectable and industrious man. With three healthy sons, and the additional income from subletting part of their home to a lady called Elizabeth Woodland, all seemed well.

Unfortunately, Sarah began to believe that her children were ill – she thought that they were suffering from scrofula, a condition which caused a swelling of the lymph nodes associated with tuberculosis. She borrowed a book on the subject from Elizabeth Woodland and regularly remarked how worried she was about her children's illness. She was so concerned that she consulted a surgeon from Fulham called Edward Tippett who examined the children and reassured her that her concerns were unfounded. However, Sarah was not consoled and believed that the children were suffering and would eventually die from the disease.

The fifteenth of November 1855 was a particularly foggy day in London. Sarah and her two younger children were out for the afternoon and had not returned when six-year-old Willie returned from school. Finding his mother absent from home, he knocked on Elizabeth Woodland's door and sat in her room until Sarah returned at 5.30 pm. Telling her tenant that she had to run an errand, Sarah went out into the foggy evening carrying baby Arthur with Willie and Edward walking by her side. Her husband William missed seeing them leave by only 15 minutes as he arrived home before six o'clock.

Nobody saw Sarah throw her children into the River Thames but several men who worked on the river heard their cries and the splashing of water and rushed to assist them. John James Godby, a waterman at the Cadogan Pier, Chelsea managed, with the assistance of a boat hook, to pull 11-month-old Arthur out of the water. He took him to the nearby Magpie and Stump public house where attempts were made to revive him. At a similar time, Joseph Reynolds, a waterman's apprentice who lived in Chelsea, pulled three-year-old Edward from under the bow of his boat before his body entered the deep water beyond Battersea Bridge. Edward was also taken to the Magpie and Stump where he was placed in a warm bath and successfully revived from his ordeal in the water. The children were recognised and their father was sent for. Arriving at the public house in a state of shock, he took his sons to the workhouse infirmary where further unsuccessful attempts were made to help baby Arthur.

Sarah Allen kept walking until she arrived at the home of a friend, Elizabeth Richards, a domestic servant who lived in Cirencester Place,

Fitzroy Square. Looking despondent, distressed and in floods of tears, she stated 'I have lost my children'. Persuading her to return home, Elizabeth Richards went with her. Her husband was lying on the bed cradling his young son Edward in his arms. He asked his wife where their eldest son Willie was but Sarah refused to answer. She began to cry, 'Where is my baby? Why can't I have my baby?' Repeated requests about Willie fell on deaf ears.

Sarah was arrested the following morning by Police Inspector Thomas Drake and taken into custody. Drake also asked her about the whereabouts of Willie but she was only able to ask for baby Arthur. Sarah was tried at Westminster Police Court later the same day. Reported to be of a very respectable and genteel appearance, she was charged on suspicion of having killed her eldest son Willie, attempting to kill her second son Edward and having drowned her baby, Arthur, by throwing all three children into the Thames.

Three days later, on 18 November 1855, Philip Parker, a horse keeper, found the body of a boy in the river 30 yards from Vauxhall Bridge. Willie had been found.

Two appearances before the Police Court at Westminster in November, and her release on the surety of £30 bail not forthcoming, Sarah spent two months in Newgate Prison before her trial at the Old Bailey before Baron Martin on 7 January 1856. Her state of mind at the time of her children's deaths was examined and evidence was provided by both her surgeon, Edward Tippett, and Dr George Roberts Rowe, the author of a work on nervous diseases. Dr Rowe told the court that Sarah's delusions of ill-health in her children was very likely the cause of her belief they would be better off dead. This view was shared by John Rowland Gibson, the surgeon of Newgate Prison who had seen Sarah every day since she had been admitted. Both men believed that Sarah had been unable to distinguish right from wrong at the time she committed the act. As a result, she was found to be insane and ordered to be detained until Her Majesty's pleasure be known.

Sarah was admitted to Bethlehem from Newgate Prison on 19 February 1856. The medical staff described her insanity as 'melancholia' due to 'over-lactation' following the birth of Arthur – the effects of which caused delusions that her children were ill. They found her to be an interesting and amiable woman who had led an exemplary life until mental instability had struck.

She was initially well behaved at Bethlehem and did not show the slightest symptom of insanity. However, following her admission she became increasingly morose and dissatisfied with her position and regularly taunted other patients about their crimes. Isolated and unsettled within the hospital, she was one of the first patients to be transferred to Broadmoor, where her mental health improved dramatically and enquiries were made about her release to her family. William, was contacted at his address in Bennetts Hill, Doctors Common, London to enquire whether he would be prepared to provide her with a home. This request upset William as he had not fully recovered from the deaths of his sons and was concerned that his remaining child may come to harm if his mother moved back to the family home. As a result, he declined to take his wife back. Sarah's sister, Ann Bessix, who was recently widowed, discovered that her brother-in-law had refused Sarah a home and agreed to provide accommodation for her in Clifton, Bristol. As a result, Sarah was released from Broadmoor on 28 August 1872, deemed to be sane.

Mary McNeill

Like Sarah Allen, Mary McNeill was an amiable, pre-possessing mother of three children who lived at 17, Murray Street, Shoreditch, London. Despite having no man in her life – the father of her two youngest children having disappeared earlier in the year – Mary lived in comfortable circumstances as she sub-let the upstairs part of her home to tenants, the Pickering family.

In September 1855, the Pickerings began to notice a change in Mary's behaviour and conduct. Her kind attentive attitude towards her children changed and she became ill-tempered and hasty with them. She frequently complained that her children had nothing to wear despite them being well dressed and on one occasion was so distressed that she threatened to throw her young baby Edwin down the stairs. The father of her eldest child, Harriet, removed his daughter from the household, leaving Mary alone with her two sons, George, aged four years, and Edwin, aged four months.

Mrs Eleanor Pickering believed that Mary was suffering from 'milk fever', an infection resulting in pain when breastfeeding. George John Amsden, a medical practitioner who had attended Mary during her confinement, was called to see her on 23 September 1855. He found her to be in a state of great nervous depression and extreme excitement as a result of having exhausted herself by nursing baby Edwin. He advised that she should not be left alone.

On the morning of Friday, 30 November 1855, Henry Charles Pickering, found Mary's cash box and a piece of her dress lying across the stairs.

Concerned that the cash box was in an unsafe place, he knocked on Mary's door and asked if she was awake. As he pushed open the door he saw baby Edwin lying on the bed covered with blood. Mary McNeill was hiding behind the door crying, 'What have I done?'. Alarmed, Henry Pickering ran into the street and called for assistance. Policeman Edwin Thompson heard his cries and accompanied him into the house where they found both George and Edwin dead on their beds – their throats had been cut with the razor that was kept locked in a kitchen drawer.

Mary was taken to the police station. Police surgeon William Henry Coward examined the bodies of her children and confirmed that their throats had been cut with a razor. At Worship Street Police Court, Mary was charged with murder and remanded in custody at Newgate Prison. Completely stricken with grief, she was removed from the court in a cab.

Mary was tried at the Old Bailey on 7 January 1856 – the same day as Sarah Allen for the same offence. Both women had been in Newgate together awaiting trial. Prison surgeon, John Rowland Gibson, gave evidence at both trials. He held the opinion that Mary was of unsound mind at the time she committed the murders. Her mother, Catherine McNeill, also gave evidence and informed the court that Mary's father had been sent to Grove Hall Institution in Stratford-le-Bow, Middlesex, six years earlier due to his deranged mind and a suicide attempt by cutting his throat. He subsequently spent time in Bethlehem but 'recovered'.

Mary McNeill was found not guilty of murder due to insanity and was ordered to be detained in a lunatic asylum until Her Majesty's pleasure be known. She was admitted to Bethlehem from Newgate Prison on 1 February 1856 – the same day as Sarah Allen. For the next 18 years, the two women would be incarcerated together, first in Bethlehem and then in Broadmoor. Mary would never be released and died in Broadmoor on 31 December 1885 of cancer of the stomach.

Chapter 4

The first male patients

Many of the earliest male patients admitted to the Criminal Lunatic Department at the General Prison of Perth in Scotland were considered to be congenital idiots and imbeciles. These individuals were unlikely to be released back into their own community.

John Jameson

The first patient admitted to Perth was John Jameson from Lerwick in the Shetland Islands, a young boy categorised as mischievous, dangerous, and a naturally dumb imbecile. John was the illegitimate son of John Jameson, a sailor, and Barbara Georgeson and was born in Lerwick about 1837. When he was three-years-old, he and his destitute mother sought board and lodgings in return for work with a widow residing in Silwick on the west coast of Mainland, Shetland. John and his mother remained there for four years but, as he matured, it became obvious that John had a learning impairment. He could hear and understand, but chose not to speak, and his behaviour became troublesome and mischievous. Despite being corrected, he appeared unable to learn from his mistakes. His mother was asked to send John back to the care of his father in Lerwick in order to keep her job.

John's father had little control over him and he became a public nuisance. He ran wild about the town playing all sorts of mischievous tricks, breaking windows and throwing dirt and other missiles into shops and at people. On several occasions, he pushed children into the sea by charging at them when they were standing on the pier. The Procurators Fiscal urged John's father to take better care of him and keep him out of mischief, but with no effect.

A warrant was issued to apprehend John to be tried at the Sheriff Court in Lerwick on 17 January 1845 for his crimes. This resulted in his committal to the local jail at Fort Charlotte pending further investigation. Although only eight years old, he was held there for three days. The Kirk Session agreed to take charge of him for one month, removing him from the area and placing him with a trustworthy guardian to watch strictly over his behaviour and prevent him from giving the public any further annoyance. The townspeople had a period of respite before he once again returned to live amongst them.

On his return to Lerwick in March 1845, John's tormenting behaviour continued. He was again brought to the Sheriff Court on 5 May 1845 but was deemed not fit for trial. In the public interest, he needed to be removed to a place of safety. Initially he was returned to Fort Charlotte before eventually being sent to the Royal Lunatic Asylum at Gartnavel, Glasgow on 21 August 1845.

While there, John was described 'as restless, tricky, mischievous and annoying as it is possible for a boy of his age to be. He seems to understand every word that is said to him although he cannot pronounce one word correctly'. John may have been an elective mute. He broke windows, tore up clothing – not just his own – and hit himself. In July 1846, John was restrained in a dark room for several hours after breaking window panes. He was transferred to Perth when it first opened on Christmas Day 1846, spending the rest of his life there. He died in 1879 from pneumonia.

William Keillor

William Keillor was born in 1828 in the village of Guildtown of St Martin's, six miles north-east of Perth. In 1844, he was awarded an apprenticeship in the painting and decorating trade in Glasgow but returned home after 18 months as 'he went wrong in the mind'. Following this breakdown, he developed a great antipathy towards his father and frequently hit him.

William Keillor was admitted to James Murray's Royal Lunatic Asylum near Perth on 17 April 1846 after assaulting his father. Within five months he was removed by the parochial Inspector of Poor, Charles Marshall, who wanted to substitute William's asylum place for another more violent patient – thus saving the parish the expense of providing maintenance for two lunatics. William returned to his family on 30 September 1846, considered 'quiet and harmless'. William Malcom, Physician to the Murray Asylum, wrote:

> 'William Keillor shewed no symptoms of violence while in the Asylum, but was a mere drivelling idiot. I would not liberate him as perfectly safe because I hold that no insane man is so.'

Within six weeks of his discharge, William was striking his father again. At a meeting of St Martin's Parochial Board on 1 July 1847, Charles Marshall was instructed to find a suitable asylum place for him.

Due to asylum overcrowding, Marshall was unable to obtain a place 'at a reasonable price' and William remained at home. A neighbour, John Garner, a blacksmith, was frequently called to restrain William and had to tie him up on many occasions to prevent him hitting his father. By March 1848, Garner had had enough and took William to the Police Office in Perth and had him apprehended for assaulting his father who was on his deathbed. The Procurator Fiscal of Perth demanded that Marshall should find Keillor a place in an asylum. On 20 March 1848, Keillor was admitted to Aberdeen Royal Asylum 'in a state of acute dementia characterised by attacks of excitement and of uncleanly habits'.

Many lunatics were 'boarded out' in Scotland. This was not only a cost-saving exercise on the poor rates payable by parishes, but also a way of providing people who needed care, and not necessarily asylum care, the opportunity to rehabilitate within a family setting. In September 1849, Charles Marshall arranged that William Keillor should return to St Martin's as a harmless and incurable lunatic – a view agreed by Dr John Forbes Ogilvie, Physician of Aberdeen Royal Asylum. William was initially boarded out on 30 September 1849 under the care of John Scott at Cattie in the parish of Old Meldrum near Inverurie, Aberdeenshire. This arrangement was satisfactory until May 1850 when John Scott raised concerns that Keillor had frightened his grandchildren by running around naked amongst them and his wife wanted him to be removed.

Under the Poor Law system, boarding out did not solely apply to harmless lunatics who were deemed to be safe. It applied to any individual who became the responsibility of the Parish, including the illegitimate children of parishioners. One woman who took boarders in this way was Elizabeth Young, wife of John Mellis, a labourer, residing in Carolina Place, St Martins, Perthshire. She was approached in August 1849 by Charles Marshall to board a six-month-old baby. The baby was Robert Meldrum, the illegitimate son of John Meldrum who kept a public house at Wolfhill in the neighbouring parish of Cargill. Elizabeth took charge of Robert – 'a very fine healthy child'. The arrangement worked well and in April 1850 Marshall asked the couple if they could also take charge of a young man who was insane but perfectly quiet and harmless – William Keillor. They agreed.

On the evening of 4 June 1850, William Keillor assisted John Mellis in boiling a large pot of horse meat on the stove in the Mellis house.

John's wife, Elizabeth, was sitting on a grassy bank near the front door cuddling baby Robert, lying on her knee. For no apparent reason, Keillor went outside, grabbed the baby and, holding him by the legs, smashed his head violently against the stump of a tree. He laughed as Robert's brains spilled on the ground. Screaming 'he's killed my bairn!', Elizabeth fainted.

John Mellis found the baby unconscious in his wife's arms with blood coming from his right ear. Dr John Clarke from Balbeggie was sent for, but there was little he could do. Robert died about 3 o'clock in the early hours of the next morning from multiple skull fractures. William Keillor was indicted for the murder of Robert Meldrum at the Circuit Court at Perth on 26 September 1850 before Lords Donald Mackenzie and James Ivory. On the evidence of Drs William Malcom and John Clark, who both declared him to be an idiot, it was clear that Keillor was mentally unfit for trial and he was ordered to be detained at Her Majesty's pleasure.

William Keillor was admitted to the Murray Asylum at Perth on 5 June 1850 and was transferred to the Criminal Lunatic Department on 18 June 1850 as its seventh patient. He remained there until his death on 21 April 1876, aged 48 years, from tuberculosis.

Completion of the male accommodation at Broadmoor was finalised at the beginning of 1864. There were five male blocks to only one female block but, as Broadmoor opened to women in 1863, it was essentially a female only asylum for the first nine months of its functioning life. Building work continued after the arrival of male patients and by the end of 1864, there were 200 men and 100 women incarcerated within its walls.

The first men to arrive at Broadmoor were transferred from Bethlehem on 27 February 1864. There were eight of them, ranging in age from 25 to 52 years, all deemed to be of unsound mind but not all murderers. Five of them were not detained at Her Majesty's pleasure, but had been given fixed sentences ranging from two years hard labour to ten years transportation to the colonies. The crimes of these five men were predominantly for theft although there was an arsonist named John Yeeles convicted in Taunton in 1857 and sentenced to 20 years hard labour. Two of the men were considered to be weak-minded – William Short was a deaf imbecile and Alfred Potter had dementia.

However, there were three murderers – Robert Knowlson convicted in York in 1846, John Goodall convicted in Derby in 1854 and Thomas Kirkwood convicted in York in 1860.

Robert Knowlson

In the village of Kirk Bramwith, seven miles from Doncaster a 70-year-old wheelwright, William Knowlson, who lived in a house close to the churchyard, was murdered by his son. In 1817, several members of the Knowlson family had been victims of the delusions of the so-called prophetess Johanna Southcott (1750-1814). In about 1792, Johanna became convinced that she possessed supernatural gifts – she wrote and dictated prophecies in rhyme, and then announced herself as the 'Woman of the Apocalypse' spoken of in the Book of Revelation. Despite dying in 1814, her legacy continued and her followers, referred to as 'Southcottians', were thought to have numbered over 100,000.

The Knowlson family became so obsessed with the prophetess that several of them left their village to take up residence in Ashton-under-Lyne where the Southcottians rapidly relieved them of a large sum of money. Being reduced to poverty, William Knowlson returned to Kirk Bramwith and, in 1846, was living with his wife, Ann, his 28-year-old son Robert, and his widowed daughter Nancy Chapman. Robert Knowlson's mind had become affected by the family's connection with the Southcottians, and he was considered in the village to be a 'harmless idiot'. However, having previously been considered gentle by family and friends and allowed as much freedom as he wanted, Robert's manner changed; he became wild and on several occasions neighbours had to be called to help protect his father from personal violence.

At supper on 4 May 1846, William remonstrated with his son. Robert became enraged and destroyed a table before going to his room. Early the following morning, William heard Robert smashing a clock, so he made his way downstairs to prevent further damage. A scuffle broke out and Robert smashed his father's head with the clock's lead weight. William Knowlson was found bleeding profusely and lying in a pool of blood at the bottom of the stairs. Although still alive, he did not regain consciousness.

Robert Knowlson, who had fled the house and run naked into a local pond after the attack, returned to his home and began to punch the bleeding body of his father. Several people attempted to restrain him, but he ran from room to room in a complete frenzy smashing windows as he tried to escape. Once caught, the only way to restrain him was with handcuffs and some irons used for agricultural purposes. Taken into custody by a local constable, Mr Lane, he was locked in a stable and fastened in chains to prevent his escape.

Robert was committed to trial at the assizes at York Castle charged with wilful murder. He was acquitted on the ground of insanity but detained for life in an asylum.

On 2 October 1846, he was admitted to Bethlehem from York Castle where his temper and mood varied; he was afraid to do wrong and on occasions appeared lost in his own world. He was transferred to Broadmoor on 27 February 1864 and died there on 26 May 1891 from softening of the brain. He is buried in St John the Baptist Church, Crowthorne, the nearest church to Broadmoor and the final resting place of many of its former patients.

John Goodall

John Goodall was born in 1811 in Doveridge, Derbyshire, the son of John Goodall and his wife Sarah. A mechanic by trade, John married Mary Hollingworth in Derby in 1833 but his wife died in 1838. John remarried the same year. His second wife, Mary Parkinson, was a respectable woman, the daughter of a superintendent at a mill in Milford, Derbyshire. The couple initially settled in Manchester where their three eldest children were born, Ann, William and Mary. They moved to Darley near Derby in the early 1850s and had a fourth child, Rachel in 1853.

John spent time working in America and on his return started to hear rumours about his wife's infidelity. Mary began to live in a state of fear as her husband repeatedly threatened to cut her throat. She found a knife concealed under his pillow on several occasions and in 1853 she moved back to Milford with their four children. Her father provided her with a home and an allowance.

Unhappy with the situation, John Goodall attempted to persuade Mary to return to him but she refused, telling him to marry someone else. Undeterred, John arrived in Milford on the morning of 18 April 1854, to visit his wife and children. While Mary was hanging some washing on the clothes line, she heard one of the children making a curious noise. Running to the house she discovered her husband coming out of an upstairs room where her youngest child, Rachel, was sleeping. He informed her 'your baby is in Heaven' and entering the bedroom she saw her 18-month-old daughter lying on the bed, her throat severed by a razor.

Goodall was seized by some local men and handed to the Milford constable who placed him in the local lock-up. An inquest was heard the following day before the coroner, Henry Mozley. John Goodall admitted that he had not felt right since the departure of his wife and family. Despite making a good home for them and pleading that they return, his wife had refused to do so. He claimed that the Lord had made him murder his little daughter and he also wanted him to kill himself. He was committed to the county gaol before being tried for wilful murder.

The trial was held at the Crown Court, Derby on 28 July 1854 before Mr Justice Maule. Several witnesses were produced who testified to John Goodall's insanity and some declared that other members of his family also suffered from similar mental health disorders. Despite evidence from other witnesses that Goodall was not insane, the jury returned a verdict of not guilty on the ground of insanity and the judge ordered that he should be detained at Her Majesty's pleasure.

Goodall was transferred from Derby Prison to Bethlehem on 20 December 1854. Described as 'very irritable', he was under the belief that people were trying to poison him by lacing his food. He was reserved and spent a lot of time in his room reading his Bible which he carried with him everywhere. A year after his arrival at Bethlehem he began to show indications of additional insanity when he insisted on calling himself by royal titles and addressing letters to his family as 'Prince John Goodall'. He believed that he had been given power from Heaven to property and to assume a variety of different prestigious titles.

Goodall was transferred along with seven other men to Broadmoor on 27 February 1864. On 11 April 1885, he attempted suicide by tying a piece of string tightly around his neck while he was in the closet on ward number 3. He was found by a warder lying on the floor, and, although apparently unhurt, was transferred to the infirmary where he remained until he died of pericarditis in 1892, aged 87 years.

His wife Mary and her three remaining children, moved to live with her elderly father, William Parkinson in Milford, where they all worked in the local cotton factory. Mary died in 1866 in Derbyshire.

Thomas Kirkwood

Thomas Kirkwood was born in Hull in 1829, son of Stephen Kirkwood, a merchant, and his wife Hannah. In the 1850s, he joined the army and served with the 29th Regiment of Foot in India. By 1860, he was home on leave and initially spent time with his sister, Mrs Todd, in Hull. While there, he made the acquaintance of Elizabeth Ann Parker, a young widow, living with her mother, Ann Sleight. Outstaying his welcome at his sister's, and overstaying his leave of absence from the army, he took lodgings with Mrs Sleight and her daughter, Elizabeth.

In April 1860 the Sleights heard a rumour that he was absent without leave from the army and asked him to go. He then went to lodge with a family called Taylor but continued to call at Mrs Sleight's home to see Elizabeth. On the morning of the 23 April 1860, he arrived there at 8am and stayed for about three hours talking with Elizabeth. At 11am he left to visit their neighbours Mr and Mrs Burnham to smoke his pipe before returning to say goodbye. As he bent to kiss Elizabeth, he put his arm around her neck and cut her throat with a razor.

Elizabeth shouted twice for Mrs Burnham and also cried out 'murder!'. Mrs Burnham looked out of her door and saw Kirkwood and Elizabeth scuffling together – she having her hand on his shoulder to prevent him getting away. Bleeding profusely from the wound to her neck, Elizabeth lacked strength and Kirkwood made his escape. A doctor was called but there was little he could do to assist her. The wound to the left side of her neck was about four inches long and she was exhausted through loss of blood. Given brandy and beef tea she passed away by 5 pm. Before dying, she gave a statement saying there was no quarrel with Kirkwood and he had said nothing before attacking her. She was unaware of any motive for the attack.

Thomas Kirkwood was apprehended shortly afterwards in a very drunken state and taken to the Mansion House 'where he acted like an infuriated madman, stoutly protesting his innocence'. Too drunk to be taken before the magistrates that day, he was remanded the following morning when he was committed for trial at the next York Assizes in July 1860. Standing before James Plaisted Wilde, 1st Baron Penzance, Thomas Kirkwood, aged 30 years, was charged with the wilful murder of Elizabeth Ann Parker. The jury, after an absence of nearly an hour, returned into court with a verdict of not guilty on the ground of temporary insanity and Kirkwood was ordered to be detained at Her Majesty's pleasure.

On 17 October 1860, Kirkwood was admitted to Bethlehem from York Prison. On arrival, it was noted that he did not show any signs of insanity. Kirkwood informed the asylum staff that he had feigned madness in order to escape the hangman, as a man named James Atkinson had successfully managed to escape the noose for a similar crime by pleading insanity in July of the previous year. Atkinson was also a patient at Bethlehem. Kirkwood was well behaved and in good health and asylum staff noted that the cause of his insanity was due to the 'heat of the climate in India'. He was transferred to Broadmoor on 27 February 1864 and died there on 20 October 1883 of pleurisy and pericarditis.

Following the death of her daughter, Ann Sleight moved into lodgings in Hull and died there in 1872 at the age of 83 years.

The men trickled into Broadmoor over the remainder of the year, arriving in groups of eight patients at a time every three to five days until about 200 men, considered to be criminally insane, had been rehoused in their new accommodation. The second consignment of men arrived on 2 March 1864. These included a French cabinet maker, Auguste Widmer, who could not speak a word of English and had been convicted of house breaking in 1860 and William Wells, a 26-year-old pianoforte maker, who is likely to have been the first patient to die at Broadmoor as he did so just three months after he was admitted. The third group of men arrived on 5 March 1864 and included William Henry Whitworth.

William Henry Whitworth

William Henry Whitworth was born in Ancoats, Lancashire in 1821. At the age of 39, he was married with children and was an acting sergeant in the Royal Artillery stationed at Sandown Fort in the Isle of Wight where he held the position of master gunner. His wife, Martha, and children, lived with him in army quarters.

William Whitworth had enlisted in the Royal Regiment of Artillery in 1840 in Manchester and accompanied his regiment to Canada later the same decade. In 1847, he married Martha Beach in Kingston, Ontario while he was based at Fort Henry and their eldest child Mary Ann, was born there two years later. In about 1850, he was serving with the 3rd Brigade at Cobh of Cork in Ireland. While there, he fell over some rocks on the coast injuring himself so badly that he was discharged from active service. Remaining in the army, he was attached to the Invalid Branch of the Artillery, filling various minor posts entrusted to men of his grade. In 1859, on account of his general good conduct and the useful services he had rendered, he was appointed master gunner at the small Sandown Fort. Captain Manners and Lieutenant Brigstock with three private soldiers who were officers' servants and belonged to the Isle of Wight Militia Artillery were also resident there. Corporal Eastley of the Royal Engineers and his wife Emma Jane, and the

Whitworths, now with six children, (Mary Ann aged eleven, Elizabeth aged nine, Frederick aged five, Ellen aged four, William aged two and Robert sixteen months) made up the remaining inhabitants.

Whitworth and his family appeared to live on the best of terms but at times his conduct suggested that the head wounds that had occurred during his fall in Ireland were impairing his mind. However, there was no indication that he would harm either himself or anyone else. On 18 May 1860, he was spotted acting strangely near the fort by some guardsmen. Holding his hands to his throat, and moaning he ran into the barrack yard in an excited state, threw himself on his knees, and, addressing Captain Robinson, said, 'For God's sake, Sir, preserve me he has used me dreadfully: he held a pistol to my head, and threatened to shoot me if I didn't cut my throat'. As there was blood on the collar of his coat he was taken to the hospital where he said, 'My wife is a good woman, I have nursed her for a fortnight, and she has nursed me, we were a loving family'.

Captain Robinson and Sergeant Dash of the Isle of Wight Militia Artillery hurried to Whitworth's quarters to check on his wife and children and were met with what amounted to wholesale slaughter. As they followed bloody footprints up the stairs, it was clear that some of the children had tried to escape the kitchen area pursued by their attacker. The floor of the main bedroom was covered with blood, papers, and articles of children's clothing, and a razor and cutlass had been abandoned on the floor – both were covered with blood. Whitworth's wife, Martha, lay on the bed with her throat gashed so severely that the bones of the vertebrae in her neck were visible. A small child lay across her lap and had been placed at the breast. On the same bed were the bodies of two other children, Whitworth's eldest son and one of his daughters. Three of his other children were lying dead on another bed with looks of horror on their faces.

Whitworth was taken into custody and treated for the wound in his neck which was not life threatening. Captain Whichcote Manners, who was in charge of the fort, gave evidence at the subsequent coroner's enquiry that Sergeant Whitworth was an odd man who always had a grievance against the other officers and claimed to possess forged documents which could have them transported. He stated that Whitworth had a great desire to remain at the fort to complete his time of service which he would have done within the next nine months – entitling him to a full pension.

Robert Henry Leeson, a surgeon practising at Sandown, also gave evidence at the coroner's inquest which made it clear that Whitworth had a severe cut across the throat made with a blunt instrument, but he thought it was done with the right hand, and was self-inflicted. Dr Leeson also examined the bodies of Whitworth's family explaining in detail the hideous wounds that had been inflicted. The coroner's jury returned a guilty verdict against William Whitworth for the wilful murder of his wife and children. He was tried at Hampshire Assizes at Winchester on 11 July 1860 and ordered to be detained at Her Majesty's pleasure due to insanity.

The bodies of his wife and children were buried in Brading Churchyard by Newport Union after the police had applied to them to organise the funeral. Seven boxes which could not have been described as coffins were provided but most proved to be too small to take the bodies without a great deal of force being applied to ensure they could be closed. It was widely felt that all was organised with sacrilegious disrespect and the deceased were not even wrapped in funeral clothes. A small party of men of the Militia Artillery arrived at Brading, and without their assistance the makeshift coffins would not have been taken into church. The service was well attended by local people, horrified and curious to witness such a gruesome spectacle, but no family member was present. Martha and her six young children were buried in a grave that was barely three feet deep.

William Whitworth was transferred from Hampshire County Prison to Bethlehem on 30 July 1860. He was considered to be both dangerous and suicidal, a widower and father to six children, all dead. The medical officers at Bethlehem recorded that Whitworth was showing possible symptoms of General Paralysis of the Insane, a condition which was caused by end stage syphilis. His speech and walk were affected and his memory impaired. His case notes reveal that he was 'a particularly amiable man with much sensitivity of feeling who frequently wept when any of the circumstances of his life were alluded to'. While at Bethlehem, another patient, Captain Campbell befriended him and took a lot of trouble to ease his mind and keep him occupied. This friendship helped improve his mind and memory. On 29 January 1861, the medical officers recorded that his mind was free from all delusions and the symptoms of General Paralysis had disappeared, suggesting a misdiagnosis. Whitworth occupied his days reading and copying extracts from books and periodicals. By July of that year, he began to express dissatisfaction at being detained as a criminal lunatic and hoped for a speedy release. Whitworth was transferred from Bethlehem on 29 August 1862 to Fisherton House Asylum in Wiltshire.

On 14 January 1864, following many complaints and difficulties in managing him at Fisherton, he was transferred back to Bethlehem. Whitworth remained convinced that he should have been discharged and as a result was litigious and made frequent unfounded complaints against the asylum attendants.

He arrived at Broadmoor on 5 March 1864. Three years later, his brother James, who lived in Ancoats, Manchester, petitioned the Home Secretary for William's release but was informed that although he was in good health physically, he remained of unsound mind. While in Broadmoor, William tried to claim an army pension but was initially informed that as he had been struck off the strength of the Royal Artillery on 14 September 1860 he was not entitled to any pension for past service as he was 'not discharged on completion of service'. The War Office later changed their minds and granted him a pension of one shilling and six pence a day for life. The following year, William's sister, Esther Ann Whitelegg wrote to the medical superintendent stating that all the correspondence she had received from her brother appeared to be that of a sane man and that she and his other relatives were willing to take care of him if he were released. A note from the medical superintendent reported that William did not show any prominent indications of insanity, but it was unlikely to be in the interests of public safety to release him.

William Whitworth died in Broadmoor on 9 May 1909 from senile decay. His family were informed of his demise and replied that they would have liked to have attended his funeral but due to their advanced ages and the huge distance from Manchester to Broadmoor they were unable to do so.

Chapter 5

Assaults on medical superintendents

The medical superintendents of asylums were qualified medical practitioners who also acted as hospital administrators. Not only charged with looking after the patients, they took on the responsibility of running their institutions and managing the staff. The superintendent had to examine all patients on arrival at the asylum and classify them according to their type of insanity. They were required to make daily visits to all parts of the asylum and random night visits. Assisted by a deputy superintendent and a medical officer, they worked closely with the matron, their team of attendants, the asylum chaplain, the schoolmaster and scores of other employees.

Asylum medical superintendents were obliged to report at least annually to their Council of Management and to the Lunacy Commission, where they were required to list their failures and shortcomings – but this also gave them the opportunity to voice their opinions for improvements.

Working in an asylum was considered to be a dangerous occupation and many of the male attendants came from a military background. However, the medical superintendents were perceived as figures of authority and many were targeted by patients who believed they were being held against their will.

Broadmoor

The first medical superintendent of Broadmoor was Dr John Meyer. He was appointed in 1862 and took up his post the following year. Eighteen months later, and only four months after Broadmoor began to take male patients, a felon named John Hughes, widely described in the press as 'a dangerous lunatic', was transferred there from Bethlehem where he had been admitted on 10 June 1859 from Newgate Prison.

John Hughes

John Hughes was born on 22 January 1822 in Camberwell, London. In 1859, he was charged with unlawfully and maliciously damaging a picture and several monuments in the parish church of Saint Marylebone and with illegally damaging two statues in the portico of the Colosseum in the parish of St Pancras.

Hughes was not unfamiliar with asylum life, having previously been admitted to Hanwell Asylum on 3 March 1857 where he was described as 'reserved, suicidal and violent'. His paramour, Sarah Mills, gave a description of his condition to the medical superintendent at the time of his admission. She stated that he was single, had one child, was able to read and write and was a member of the Church of England.

Hughes was good at his job and had been in constant employment as a chair-maker but had always had a violent temperament. Over Christmas 1856, he began wandering the streets by night and day carrying an axe in his pocket and a Bible in his hand. After a week, he returned home and began to destroy furniture and crockery in the house. He sang and danced and was very violent, standing over Sarah waving an axe. He was approached by the police when he exposed himself at the window. His language was abusive and violent towards them, and in order to restrain him they had to break a door down. He was removed to a workhouse and cared for until he had calmed down and was discharged a month later. Within a fortnight of his release, he set his house on fire and was once again admitted to the workhouse.

His brother also provided information to the asylum authorities. He informed the medical superintendent that John had received a head injury when he was 15 years old and was treated at the Middlesex Hospital for six weeks. Following this injury, he developed a violent temper. He ran away from his apprenticeship and enlisted in the 24th Regiment of Infantry but was bought off by his mother after serving two years. Following his discharge, he joined the police force but was dismissed after a year. He then entered the Fire Escape Brigade but was also dismissed from service.

Before his illness, Hughes was not in the habit of attending church or reading the Bible and he had refused to marry Sarah Mills, the mother of his child, with whom he lived saying that 'marriage was an unnecessary form and a mere ceremony'.

He was discharged from Hanwell Asylum in November 1858 against the advice of the medical superintendent who remained unconvinced about his sanity. Hughes was very coherent in conversation and wrote many letters to the asylum committee requesting his discharge. The committee believed him to be sane and recommended he be removed on probation.

On the evening of 31 March 1859, bell-toller Henry Arthur closed the Parish Church of St Marylebone after the last service. The following morning, he was alerted that the vestry door had been forced, the cords of the window had been cut and pushed open about two feet. Entering the church, he saw that several of the monuments had been defaced with graffiti. Lord Teignmouth's monument had been inscribed with 'Not wanted here'. The head of Colonel Fitzgerald's monument had been defaced and the words 'Learn your horses to smoke; you have made asses of yourselves' – a picture of a horse's head smoking a pipe had been added to the monument. A picture had been inscribed with the words 'Learn to worship God and destroy rubbish' which were scratched into the varnish.

On 9 May 1859, 37-year-old Hughes stood trial at the Old Bailey for maliciously damaging a picture and several monuments in the church. At his trial, several attendants from Hanwell Asylum gave evidence that Hughes was in the habit of writing on the walls and also in Bibles and other reading materials that were available for the patients. They confirmed that the writing matched that of Hughes. Dr William Bailey, Physician of the Hanwell Lunatic Asylum informed the court that he believed Hughes was insane.

His common-law wife and her mother, Sarah and Ellen Mills, also gave evidence about his handwriting. These testimonies corroborated evidence that the writing on the walls and documents in the church had been made by Hughes. As each witness spoke against him, Hughes berated them declaring them to be unfit to give evidence.

He was declared to be not guilty on the ground of insanity and was ordered to be detained during Her Majesty's pleasure.

Shortly after his arrival at Broadmoor, Hughes believed that the medical superintendent, Dr Meyer, had accused him of 'murdering the Queen of Heaven'. Determined to avenge the insult, he aimed a blow at him with a heavy flint slung in a handkerchief during Divine Service in the Asylum Chapel in March 1866. The force of the blow was lessened by an officer named Woodhouse, who seized Hughes, but Dr Meyer received a very ugly wound to the right side of his head, the effects of which he felt until his death a few years later. After the attack, Dr Meyer noted in the Medical Superintendent's Journal, 'it is a mercy that I am here to write this account of the occurrence'.

John Hughes died on 19 September 1893 of softening of the brain. He spent the last three months of his life in the asylum infirmary. His death was widely reported in the national press; 'Broadmoor has lost its most dangerous inmate'.

Dr William Orange succeeded Dr John Meyer as the second medical superintendent of Broadmoor in May 1870. Following Meyer's early departure due to ill-health after Hughes' attack, Orange fulfilled the role of acting medical superintendent while still the deputy. He was therefore responsible for the running, administration and care of the patients when a felon named Henry Leest was admitted to Broadmoor in 1869.

Henry Leest

Henry Leest was born on 19 December 1844 in the parish of All Saints, Norwich, the son of Edward Leest, a cordwainer, and his wife, Mary Ann Gooch. Henry was a slight man with a swarthy complexion and his limbs were badly scarred. Like his father, by trade he was a shoemaker. Following his father's death in 1858, the family initially remained in Norwich but by the mid-1860s, Mary Ann and several of her children including Henry had moved to London.

Once in the capital, Leest embarked on a career of petty crime. Living a nomadic existence, his first criminal conviction in 1864 was for vagrancy which led him to Holloway Prison for three months. The following year he was convicted twice, spending nearly seven months in prison for theft and vagrancy and, in 1866, he spent an additional two periods in prison for theft and drunkenness.

On 26 March 1867, Leest entered a post office in Deptford and stole 22 shillings in cash and 6 shillings worth of postage stamps. He was committed to the prison at Greenwich to await trial which took place at Maidstone on 11 April of the same year. Convicted of larceny, Leest was sentenced to five years penal servitude which he initially spent at Millbank Prison.

In November 1867, he threatened to commit suicide and the staff at Millbank placed him in a strait jacket to prevent him carrying out his threat. He also began to feign insanity which was not believed by staff who claimed him to be an imposter. He was moved to Portsmouth Prison on 22 January 1868, but his behaviour began to deteriorate, and he made another feigned attempt to commit suicide by trying to cut his throat.

Transferred back to Millbank Prison in 1869, he was found to be suffering from syphilis and was deemed to be of unsound mind. His mother, Mary Ann, who lived in Pimlico, visited him on a couple of occasions accompanied by his siblings.

On 29 October 1869, Leest was transferred to Broadmoor. On arrival, he was noted to be filthy in his habits, mischievous, and a man who 'seized every opportunity of committing self-abuse'. His syphilitic ulcers were treated with an iodide of potassium application. Once again, he attempted suicide and spent many hours in seclusion due to his destructive and aggressive behaviour. He attacked both the principal attendant and also Broadmoor's new deputy medical superintendent, Dr William Douglas, who had only been in post for four months. Dr Douglas was so badly hurt that he resigned from his position and took up a safer career in general practice in Newbury, Berkshire about 30 miles from Broadmoor.

On 14 August 1871, having become more mentally stable and therefore allowed more freedom, Leest was allowed to help with the summer harvest digging potatoes. Asking permission of the watchful attendant, Leest went to answer a call of nature, taking with him the basket he had been using to store the newly picked crop. With the aid of the basket he was able to reach the top of the external wall and climbing quickly over it made his way into nearby woods. A pursuit followed but staff were not able to catch him.

The authorities informed Leest's mother and brothers of his escape and were told by one of his brothers that he had received a letter from him postmarked Winchester. Assuming that he was heading for either the port of Southampton or Portsmouth, attendants were despatched to hunt him down. They found him six days later waiting to board a ship to New York. In the week of his escape, he had managed to find work and had his wages with him. Henry's brother Walter had emigrated to America in 1870 and was living in Massachusetts which is perhaps where he was heading.

Far from ensuring his further incarceration, Dr Orange formed the opinion that if Leest was capable of carrying out such a plan and was employable then he was clearly sane. As a result, he was transferred back to Millbank Prison. Once back in London, his mother and two brothers were able to visit him which they did on 7 October 1871. On 2 November 1871, he was released on licence five months early. He gave his release address as 86, Tachbrook Street, Pimlico.

Henry Leest moved to America in the 1870s, writing to Dr Orange at Broadmoor to tell him that he had been shuttling between Rhode Island and Boston but asking the superintendent for money because he was down on his luck. It is likely that Dr Orange, who was a firm believer in extending care to former patients, sent him money to help him out.

Henry's mother, Mary Ann, was admitted to Woking Lunatic Asylum on 8 February 1879 and died there three years later on 30 July 1882.

Reverend Henry John Dodwell

Henry Dodwell was born in Shepperton, Middlesex, on 7 October 1825, the son of Edward (a solicitor) and Anne Dodwell. Henry and his older brothers, Edward and George, were pupils at Bedford Grammar School. Henry then went to Exeter College, Oxford, where he studied until 1848, when he graduated Bachelor of Arts. His elder brother, George Branson Dodwell, attended St John's College, Cambridge. Both brothers were ordained – George in 1845 and Henry in 1859.

Henry began his working life as an assistant master at Bedford Grammar School and by 1861 appears to have opened a school in Kensington as he was described as a curate and tutor on the decennial census. On 23 July 1866, Henry married Eliza Dunn, who was twenty years younger than him, at St Martin-in-the-Fields, Westminster, and the couple had four children, two sons and two daughters all of whom were born in Brighton.

In the late 1860s, Henry Dodwell became Chaplain to the Brighton Industrial Schools as well as continuing to tutor maths and classical studies. Dodwell was asked to vacate his position at the Industrial Schools, but declining, the Local Government Board ordered that he be removed on 15 March 1873. Feeling persecuted and ill-used by the Guardians of the school, Dodwell began a long and tedious campaign to have himself reinstated. In need of employment, he became a schoolmaster at an endowed school in Devon. However, within a short period of time, the governing body of the school dismissed him for alleged misconduct. Once again, Dodwell had no job and no home and as a result he refused to give up possession of the school-house or master's residence. The governing body of the school brought an action against him to recover possession of the house, and the case was heard in the court of Sir George Jessell, Master of the Rolls.

Dodwell engaged a solicitor to represent him but they soon quarrelled and the two parted company. Unfortunately, the solicitor's name was still on the court record which resulted in no defence being made to the court. Dodwell made an application to Sir George to set aside the judgment by default which he allowed. Failing to hire another solicitor to represent him,

Dodwell put in his own statement of defence and pleaded his case at considerable length about his perceived ill-treatment. Sir George awarded judgment against Dodwell which ensured that he was obliged to leave the school master's residence.

Dissatisfied with the decision of Sir George, Dodwell once again decided to take matters into his own hands. In 1877, he issued a petition of right to the Court of Appeal, asking to be re-instated to his post at the Brighton Schools. Once again, Sir George Jessell informed him that an order based on a petition could not be made. This decision determined Dodwell's next action. Under the belief that all his grievances would be heard if he was able to once again appear in court, he decided to shoot Sir George, a man he had come to loathe.

On 22 February 1878, he waited for him to arrive at court in Chancery Lane. As Sir George got out of his cab, Dodwell produced a pistol, pointed it towards Sir George and fired. As onlookers rushed to the scene, Dodwell went up to the judge, introduced himself, and was immediately arrested.

Initially appearing at Bow Street Magistrates Court, he was held at Newgate Prison before standing trial at the Old Bailey. He was charged with two offences – wounding and assault. The bullet from the gun was never retrieved. Dodwell later explained in court that he had stuffed a ball of paper into the barrel inscribed with the words 'Unfaithful to the true interests of the Crown of England'. Dodwell took full advantage of the ensuing court case to once again make himself appear to be a man who had suffered many grievances at the hands of others.

The jury found him not guilty on the ground of insanity and Dodwell arrived in Broadmoor on 30 March 1878. Although doubtless considered to be eccentric, there was sympathy and support against his conviction and two eminent physicians, Dr Lyttelton Stewart Forbes Winslow and Dr James Michell Winn took up his cause. This sympathy and his supporters disappeared when Dodwell decided on a final course of action to have his injustices heard.

On the evening of 6 June 1882, Dr William Orange met Dodwell for a supposedly private meeting at Dodwell's request ostensibly to discuss a letter he was writing to his brother George, who at the time was a professor of divinity living in Nova Scotia. While Dr Orange was reading the letter, Dodwell suddenly struck him forcibly on the temple with a stone wrapped in a handkerchief. The doctor was badly hurt but managed to escape the room out into the corridor where staff came to his rescue. Dodwell followed the superintendent continuing to aim further blows to his head. He was finally overpowered by two attendants. Dodwell claimed that he had a right to attack the superintendent, as Dr Orange was keeping him unlawfully detained.

Dodwell's actions had largely alienated him from his family, and his wife and children were living in fairly impoverished circumstances. His daughters, Eliza and Sarah, boarded at the Princess Mary Village Homes Institution, in Chertsey, Surrey. The school had been founded in 1870 for the children of criminal parents whose physical and moral health was threatened by the poverty and depravity of their environment. Dodwell's elder son, Henry, was boarded at the School of Emmanuel Hospital in Westminster – an establishment dating back to the late 1500s 'for the bringing up of children in virtue and good and laudable arts so that they might better live in time to come by their honest labour'. In the early 1880s, Dodwell's younger son, Edward, was living in lodgings with his mother near St Pancras in London and Eliza was making a living as a seamstress.

Henry John Dodwell died in Broadmoor on 15 June 1900 of heart failure and is buried in Woking Cemetery. His probate records show that his £200 estate was left to his wife.

The third medical superintendent of Broadmoor was Dr David Nicolson who was born in Auchlethen, Cruden, Aberdeenshire in 1844. In 1876 he was appointed Deputy Medical Superintendent at Broadmoor and seven years later he was assaulted by a patient, Henry Forrester, who had been admitted to Broadmoor on 16 July 1880 following an assault on a hospital doctor in London.

Henry Forrester

27 May 1880 began as an ordinary day at King's College Hospital, London. The assistant house physician, John Frederick William Silk, was in a consulting room administering treatment to a patient named Henry Herbert Skelton, a bookbinder from Mortimer Court, Kingsland. As Dr Silk was tending to Skelton, Henry Forrester, suffering delusions of persecution, struck Silk on the back of the head with a piece of iron resembling a poker. The blow was so violent that Silk fell to the floor insensible and did not recover for four days. Before Forrester could strike again he was grabbed by other patients in the waiting room and held until help arrived.

Forrester's delusions were complex – he believed that fire was coming from his eyelashes, and he could continually smell sulphur. He experienced burning pains all over his body and was under the impression that the doctors at the hospital were trying to poison him with medication. Taken into custody, he was sent to Clerkenwell Prison where he was examined by the prison surgeon, Dr Carpenter, who determined that he was of unsound mind. At his trial on 22 June 1880 before Frederick Flowers (1810-86) at Bow Street Police Court he was found not guilty on the ground of insanity and was admitted to Broadmoor.

In 1884, Forrester jabbed Dr Nicolson behind the ear with a stone wrapped in a handkerchief but the medical superintendent was saved from serious injury by the swift action of an attendant standing close to him. Forrester died in Broadmoor on 22 December 1913.

In 1889, Dr Nicolson was injured by another patient, James Lyons, who threw a stone which struck him on the head cutting his scalp and laying him up with concussion for ten weeks.

James Lyons (also known as James Regan, Smith, Price, Read, Baker or Caffrey)

Lyons was a petty criminal, convicted on many occasions for burglary and housebreaking and known by a number of different aliases. Born in August 1856 in Sheffield, Yorkshire, his mother Bridget attributed his odd behaviour to a fall on the head when he was three which had rendered him 'queer' and prone to temper outbursts during which he threw things. She declared there was no insanity in the family and his father had died of consumption. When James was 10 years of age, his mother married again. Her second husband was James Caffrey and the family continued to live in Sheffield.

Lyon's life of crime began when he was a teenager. On 26 March 1874, he was convicted at Leeds Assizes of burglary and housebreaking. Sentenced to seven years penal servitude, he was also ordered to three years police supervision. He began his sentence in Woking Convict Prison. On the expiration of this sentence he was transferred to Broadmoor under the name James Regan (his mother's maiden name) for three months before being removed to Wakefield Asylum on 3 May 1881.

At Leeds Quarter Sessions on 9 January 1888, he was charged with warehouse breaking and larceny. Having stolen 100lbs of leather, he was found guilty and sentenced to five years penal servitude which he initially served in Wakefield Prison. He again took up the insane ticket and wangled a transfer to Broadmoor on 19 March 1888. On 3 November the following year, he struck Dr Nicolson with a stone which caused profuse bleeding to the doctor's head after which he required a period of six weeks rest and relaxation away from his duties in order to recuperate.

In December 1892, the authorities considered moving Lyons to a district asylum near his home town of Sheffield. Menston Asylum (now High Royds Hospital) in Wakefield was the obvious choice but he was certified unfit for transfer. On 8 January 1893, his sentence expired and he ceased to be a criminal lunatic but was detained as a pauper lunatic suffering from dangerous delusions under an order of a Justice of the Peace. Sheffield Union were charged with his maintenance at 2/6 daily.

He continued his life of crime following discharge from the asylum and as late as 1933 was imprisoned for shop-breaking. When he was released from prison he gave his intended address as the Church Army Home in Sheffield but it is unclear whether he went there as he died on 4 December 1933.

Chapter 6

Idiots and imbeciles

From as early as the fourteenth century there was a clearly defined legal difference established through the judiciary of England between idiots and lunatics. This distinction was made because of the Crown's rights over land inheritance and the statute of *De Prerogativa Regis* (Royal Prerogative) dating from 1322 during the reign of Edward II. This statute protected the estates of those people who by a natural progress of mental decay became demented.

Idiots, who in the early days were termed 'natural fools', were seen as having a congenital and permanent condition involving an absence of understanding. Lunatics, on the other hand, also termed persons *non compos mentis*, acquired their lack of reasoning after birth and could have lucid intervals when they appeared to be rational. The altered state of mind of lunatics was considered legally to be a temporary illness. The Crown held royal prerogative over the wardship of the lands of natural fools, taking all the revenues from their estates but providing for their sustenance. The lands were returned to the idiot's heirs on his death. For those persons *non compos mentis*, however, the king protected the lunatic's estate and maintained them and their family with estate revenues throughout their illness. All profits from the estate reverted to the lunatic or their heirs on their recovery or death.

By the fifteenth century 'idiot' rather than 'natural fool' had become the preferred term. The new category of 'imbecile' was developed in addition to the terms 'idiot' and 'lunatic'. In Scotland, the term 'fatuous' was used as a way of describing imbecility. By the nineteenth century there was a clearly defined difference between idiots and imbeciles based on their intelligence. Someone defined as an idiot had a profound intellectual incapacity and was general considered to function at the same level as a three year old. They would have limited communication. Examples would include Down syndrome or untreated cretinism (congenital hypothyroidism). Imbeciles were people who had acquired a permanent cognitive impairment after birth maybe from causes such as a traumatic brain injury, encephalitis, meningitis, or poisoning with toxins. These individuals generally functioned mentally in the same way as a six year old. Their disabilities, although permanent, were generally not considered quite as profound as those of idiots.

The 1845 Lunatics Act defined mental incapacity in three ways. 'Lunatics' who were temporarily incapacitated but had lucid intervals; 'idiots' who had an incapacity with no intervals of sanity; and, 'persons of unsound mind' who had acquired their incapacity. Until the mid-nineteenth century, imbeciles and idiots would have been cared for firstly by their family, or failing that, by neighbours or through their local community.

The terms 'idiots' and 'imbeciles' remained prevalent into the twentieth century. Today they would be recognised as people with learning disabilities and the previous contemporary terminology is nowadays considered derogatory and offensive. Idiots and imbeciles were treated no differently by the court system than others who had committed crime. In many cases they were considered dangerous to the general public and a threat to society because of their low intellect. In Scotland, the first female patient to be admitted to the Criminal Lunatic Department at Perth in 1847 was a woman classified as an imbecile.

Mary Paterson

Mary Paterson was born on 10 April 1813 in the Scottish Borders town of Peebles. Daughter of a cotton hand-loom weaver, Robert Paterson, and his wife Jean Dickson, the family lived on the North Side of the Old Town.

On the afternoon of 18 February 1842, 12-year-old John Purves was walking home from school along the turnpike road from Peebles to Biggar. His father was a forester and the family at that time lived at Neidpath Cottage, one mile west of Peebles. Approaching home, he saw thick smoke rising and realised that the woodland near Neidpath Castle was on fire. The gorse bushes by the side of the road were burning and the fire had extended to the grass in the wood and was raging fiercely. John spotted Mary Paterson standing beside a wheel-barrow in the middle of the road – she had been gathering dung to be dried and used as fuel. She was laughing and John asked her what she had done. She told him that she had kindled the gorse with two lucifer matches but would never do it again. John raised the alarm and with the help of his mother, Mary, along with Thomas Clark, a local carter, and Robert Park, a weaver from Tweed-Bridge End, they managed to thrash out the flames and get the fire under control. Mary Paterson looked on, making no attempt to help quell the flames and continued to laugh. The fire extended to an area of almost 2,000 square yards and destroyed 200 young trees.

Mary Paterson was charged with wilful, wicked and felonious fire raising and malicious mischief. Her trial took place in the Circuit Court at Jedburgh on 4 April 1842. Thomas Clark, who had helped to put out the fire, gave evidence saying that he had known Mary for over 20 years. He stated 'I do not think she is an idiot but she has a "want" [lacked common sense]. She knows when she is doing ill. She is inclined to be mischievous and is at times devilish. I have often seen her throwing stones at people'. Medical evidence was heard from Alexander Renton and John McNab, both local surgeons. They had examined Mary in Peebles Prison on 25 February 1842 and found her of unsound mind, declaring that, having known her from infancy, they had no hesitation in pronouncing her fatuous and therefore not responsible for her actions. Mary's father, Robert Paterson, was questioned and detailed that Mary had been to school and could read a little from the Bible. However, he added that 'when any person stirs her up a little she becomes unmanageable – when she is raised up her temper becomes very violent. She has always been considered as deficient in intellect'. Mary was deemed to be insane and not fit for trial. She was ordered to be detained in prison until further orders of the Court.

Mary was admitted to the Royal Asylum of Edinburgh at Morningside in 1842 and subsequently transferred to the Criminal Lunatic Department at Perth on 23 September 1847. She remained there until 13 November 1876, when she was released with several other patients, all of whom were no longer considered to be a threat to their community. It is likely that she was transferred to a poorhouse and may have died in Edinburgh two years later.

John Yeeles

John Yeeles was also considered to be an imbecile with frequent bouts of incoherence and was admitted to Broadmoor the day it opened. Like Mary Paterson, he had also been tried and convicted of arson. In 1857 in Taunton, Devon, he set fire to two stacks of wheat and one of clover at Easton in Gordano, Devon, which was the property of George Flower. Despite being categorised as an idiot by the prison surgeon, he was sentenced to 20 years penal servitude. Yeeles was initially incarcerated in Leicester Gaol before being transferred to a prison hulk in Portsmouth in January 1859. He joined another hulk in Gibraltar on 18 July 1859.

These hulks were decommissioned and partially-dismantled warships. Stripped of their masts, rigging and sails, they were converted into makeshift prisons and were originally considered a short-term solution to alleviate the overflowing penal system. They were moored in estuaries neighbouring the Royal Naval Dockyards in Britain and were also situated in Bermuda and Gibraltar. Incarceration within them was considered to be 'hell on water' with many prisoners falling ill due to the cramped unsanitary conditions.

On 17 March 1862, the medical officer on the prison ship concluded that Yeeles 'appears always to have been idiotic. In so much so now as to render him useless to the Public Works Prison'. John Yeeles was invalided from Gibraltar on 26 March 1862 and returned to Britain where he was admitted to Millbank Prison. On admission, it was noted that he had some form of mental disorder and he was transferred to Bethlehem where a diagnosis of imbecility was made. He was able to engage in very simple conversations but made no attempt to mix with other patients or join in any occupation or amusement that was offered.

He was transferred to Broadmoor on 27 February 1864, and died there on 13 December 1872 aged 54.

Henry Constant

Henry Constant was admitted to Bethlehem on 23 October 1862 and categorised as a weak-minded man who had been an imbecile for many years. He was born in Clearwell, Gloucestershire in about 1812 and never married, living mainly with his siblings, one of whom was William. Despite being described as blind in the 1861 census, William Constant was the publican of the Butcher's Arms in Clearwell.

On Monday 9 June 1862, a club feast was held at the Butcher's Arms and Henry's siblings believed it would be easier for him to stay with friends locally as he was prone to being teased by local children. The following day Henry was morose and refused to eat. He went into a nearby field and attacked a young boy, Thomas Jones, who was picking stones from the crop. A man named Richard Matthews ran to assist the boy and told Henry to go home. Shortly afterwards, Sarah Coleman, a neighbour of the Constant family and someone who had known Henry for most of his life, heard him call a 10-year-old boy, John Cecil, to join him at the top of the field.

Both John and Mrs Coleman thought he was being called to look at some sheep and as he was a friend of the Constant family, he did not hesitate to go. Hearing screams from the field, Mrs Coleman ran to the Butcher's Arms to alert Henry's brother that there was a problem and he should send for the boy's father.

Henry Constant arrived home shortly afterwards and admitted that he had injured John Cecil. Henry's sister, unsure what to do, made her charwoman Margaret Hughes, who was at the pub cleaning up after the club dinner, go to the field to see what the matter was. Mrs Hughes discovered John Cecil badly beaten about the head, lying in his own blood and apparently dead. He was carried to his parents' home insensible and after receiving a little brandy revived slightly. However, he did not open his eyes and despite the attentions of John Hatton, surgeon of Coleford, who quickly arrived on the scene, he died the following day.

John Cecil was an intelligent little boy, eldest son of John, a labourer in the employ of the Countess of Dunraven, and his wife Sarah and much liked by Henry Constant. He had spent a great deal of his time with the Constant family and Henry's elder brother, William, called him 'my little bailiff'. There did not appear to be any motive for the crime.

At the ensuing inquest, Margaret Hughes, the charwoman who had found the body was required to give evidence. She confirmed that Henry Constant was 'not in his right mind' and 'had been silly all his life'. She gave various instances when his behaviour had been odd including him eating straw and rags. Henry Constant had been a worry to his family for about a year and they and other members of the community had kept a careful eye on his behaviour. A medical expert had been consulted and he advised that Henry be given plenty of freedom as he was not considered to be dangerous.

The coroner's jury returned a verdict of wilful murder and Henry was committed to await trial at the next assizes. Henry Constant, a grey haired old man stood in the dock in Gloucester on 12 August 1862. He was asked to plead but did not appear to understand the question and made no reply. The governor of Gloucester Gaol, Captain Cartwright, gave evidence that he had observed him every day and was of the firm opinion that he was an imbecile. This view was shared by two doctors who had also examined him after the murder and believed that he was not aware that the act he had committed was wrong. The jury found that Constant was not in a fit state to stand trial and he was ordered to be detained at Her Majesty's pleasure.

He was admitted to Bethlehem from Gloucester Gaol on 23 October 1862 where it was established that he could neither read nor write and had never undertaken any trade or employment. Seen as a 'miserable looking man, old looking for his age', the accompanying medical certificate from Gloucester Gaol stated 'Henry Constant is harmless and quiet, he seldom sleeps at night and is fanciful as to his food'. He was transferred to Broadmoor on 2 March 1864 and died there on 21 February 1879, from brain disease.

James Todman

James Todman fell into the lower category of intelligence and was considered to be an idiot. He was born in Chertsey, Surrey in 1825 the son of James Todman and his wife Sarah Head. James senior was an agricultural labourer, and by 1851, the family, which included a younger son Henry, who was also defined as an idiot, were living at Stow Hill, Chertsey.

In August 1857, James Todman junior was convicted at Croydon Assizes of sodomy with a 13-year-old boy and ordered to be detained at Her Majesty's pleasure on the ground of insanity. The actual crime was not reported in the local press and the prison records showed their abhorrence of the act by describing it as 'b*****y'.

James was committed to Horsemonger Lane Gaol in Newington, which was Surrey's principal prison and place of execution until its closure in 1878. While there, he spent time in the prison infirmary, and was locked up with three other men: John Hodges, an agent of the Birkbeck Life Assurance Company convicted of forgery; James Preston, a debtor; and Samuel Sowerby. James Preston had been sent to the prison infirmary suffering from depression.

On the night of 7 September 1857, Preston got out of bed to use the closet. When he returned he was holding a bucket in both hands which he raised and struck John Hodges forcibly about the head several times. He then took the bucket back to the closet and returned to his bed. John Hodges died of his injuries and an inquest into his death was held at which Samuel Sowerby and James Todman were called as witnesses. James Todman's appearance was widely reported in the press as being 'a most diminutive and repulsive looking dwarf who could neither read nor write'.

Todman was admitted to Bethlehem on 18 September 1857 where a more detailed description of his physical appearance was recorded:

'His appearance would at once convince a jury that his amount of intelligence was remarkably low. He is misshapen with a low retracting forehead, considerable posterior development of the cranium (with ears precisely similar to a monkey's the tips almost reaching the summit of the head).'

The staff at Bethlehem had a few problems with him during his incarceration and were obliged to keep him apart from other patients of a similar sexual orientation.

Todman had no objections to sodomy being committed on him and attempted the act with another patient defined as an idiot in March 1860. He was transferred to Broadmoor on 19 March 1864. His niece and her husband informed the medical superintendent that they were willing to find him a home if he were released, but this did not occur and James Todman died in Broadmoor on 13 March 1911 from bronchitis and senile decay.

Richard Stickler

Richard Stickler was born in 1804 in Witham Friary, Somerset, son of William and Ann Stickler. He never married and spent his life working as an agricultural labourer for his brother John, who farmed 130 acres of land at Holt Farm.

On 9 July 1862, Richard Stickler was arrested for committing an act of bestiality with 'a certain heifer' and admitted to Shepton Mallet Gaol to await trial at the next assizes. He was tried in Wells in August 1862, found guilty and sentenced to ten years penal servitude. Imprisoned in Taunton Gaol, he frequently exposed himself and sat in his cell in a state of undress. Found to be insane, he was transferred to Bethlehem on 1 October 1862 where they determined that his intellect was of 'a very low order, his head is small anteriorly and he has a repulsive countenance'.

Richard Stickler was transferred to Broadmoor on 26 March 1864 and died there on 27 November the same year from a strangulated hernia which he had suffered from since boyhood. An inquest was performed and determined that he had died from natural causes.

Thomas Cathie Wheeler

Thomas Wheeler was born in London in 1823, the son of a tailor. In the late 1840s, he spent time working in South America employed as a clerk.

Returning in 1848 aged 24, his family immediately noticed a change in him which they believed to be symptoms of insanity. He complained that he had no energy and that his insides had come out so he was obliged to hold onto things to maintain his balance. His condition did not improve and his family made the decision to request his admission to Bethlehem which he entered on 16 March 1849.

The medical staff at Bethlehem noted that he appeared to be suffering from delusions as he believed himself to be someone else – the cause of which was considered to be an over application of work although there was a history of insanity in the family with both his maternal grandmother and a paternal cousin also considered to be insane. Described by the staff as whimsical and flighty, it was difficult to engage him in any activity for long and he declared that he was unable to work as the system of treatment at Bethlehem was killing him.

He showed distinct signs of weak mindedness but his family visited him regularly, and despite not being cured, he was discharged on 7 December 1849 at the request of his mother, Elizabeth, who had been persuaded to relieve him by an aunt. This was against the advice of the medical superintendent who did not believe it would be to anyone's benefit.

His aunt decided to conduct an experiment to determine whether Thomas would improve if he lived with her, but his state of mind seemed to get worse and at the end of two weeks she gladly handed him back to his mother. In February 1850, his mother procured an order for his admission to the Surrey County Lunatic Asylum at Wandsworth where he remained for about 12 months. Yet again, he was discharged uncured and moved back to live with his mother at 1, Durham Place, Lambeth Road, which was also home to John and Eliza Tongs. The Tongs were concerned about the level of anger Thomas showed towards his mother and suggested that he should again be committed to an asylum, to which she agreed.

On 11 April 1852, Eliza Tongs and another lodger at the address, Eliza Phillips, heard a loud crash from the Wheeler rooms. Eliza Phillips knocked on their door and when it was answered by Thomas Wheeler, she asked to see his mother. His look terrified her and she ran downstairs and alerted Eliza Tongs who called her husband from his adjoining workshop. At the same time, Thomas Wheeler left the property with a coat over his shoulder and a walking stick in his hand. Knowing that he was no longer in the property, the Tongs went upstairs to check on the welfare of his mother. They were utterly unprepared for the sight that faced them. The body of a woman was lying on its stomach on the floor – its head had been completely severed and put on the table alongside the meal that Elizabeth Wheeler had prepared for her son. It was only at that point that they recognised that the deceased was Elizabeth.

John Tongs ran out into the street and alerted the first policeman that he saw, Constable Thomas Lockyer. Pointing out Thomas Wheeler, the policeman approached him and John Tongs stated, 'You've killed your mother' to which Wheeler replied, 'I know I have'. He was taken to the local police station while enquiries were made as to the extent of Elizabeth's injuries.

An inquest was held by coroner Mr W. Carter in the Three Stags Tavern on Kennington Road, London where Wheeler admitted that he had hit his mother with a flat iron before cutting her throat with a carving knife. Discovering that he was unable to sever her head with the knife, he used a hatchet to decapitate her. When he left the house, he had intended to kill himself by cutting his own throat. The jury returned a verdict of wilful murder and Thomas was taken to Horsemonger Lane Gaol to await trial at the Old Bailey.

At the ensuing trial, the surgeon at Horsemonger Lane, Dr Wintour Harris, gave evidence that Thomas was insane. He stated that he saw prisoners committed for murder on a daily basis and on every occasion that he had seen Thomas he was completely sure that he was suffering from delusions. He had expressed a wish to die and that if he was not able to do it himself he wished the law to do it for him.

A week before the trial began, Thomas Wheeler had been moved to Newgate Prison and the governor, William Wadham Cope, was also asked to give evidence to the court about his state of mind. He declared that he found Thomas to be rational but did not believe that he fully understood the difference between guilty and not guilty. The jury found Thomas Wheeler to be of unsound mind and he was ordered to be detained at Her Majesty's pleasure.

He was re-admitted to Bethlehem on 3 June 1852 where it was noted that he was quiet, orderly and contented but prone to unexplained outbursts of laughter. He took a dislike to some people and one in particular, an attendant called Hosper. One evening, as the attendant was about to serve the evening meal and carve the meat, Thomas Wheeler grabbed the knife from him and attempted to kill him in the same way that he had killed his mother. The attendant received several extensive wounds to his scalp before some patients managed to overpower Wheeler.

He was transferred to Broadmoor on 23 March 1864. On 16 December 1872, he attempted to escape. Instead of returning from the airing court at the end of the afternoon, he concealed himself in bushes on the Terrace. After dark, he jumped the perimeter wall. He was apprehended on the road to Crowthorne having been absent for four hours and taken back to the asylum. He died there on 25 January 1907 aged 83, from pneumonia.

Chapter 7

Mentally weak habitual criminals

There was concern towards the latter half of the nineteenth century about the growing increase in urban degeneration due to poverty and poor parenting. It was believed by many social commentators that the semi-criminal class of society resulted from 'physical, mental and moral peculiarities' who were tainted by inherited defects. Dr Richard Frith Quinton, former governor and medical officer of Holloway Prison, commented that 'some criminals are of bad or degenerate stock' and were 'different to skilled criminals who would not have recruited associates of low intelligence'.

This group of 'would be' criminals were defined as moral imbeciles by Sir James Crichton-Browne, son of Dr W.A.F. Browne, one of the most significant asylum doctors of the nineteenth century whose opinions and foresight led to a great many asylum reforms. Sir James determined that moral imbeciles were:

> 'persons who, by reason of arrested development or disease of the brain, dating from birth or early years, display at an early age vicious or criminal propensities, which are of an incorrigible or unusual nature, and are generally associated with some slight limitation of intellect.'

This view was agreed by George A. Auden in his work *Feeblemindedness and Juvenile Crime* (1911). Auden identified cases perpetrated by young offenders whom he identified as 'moral imbeciles' and argued that defining and detaining such individuals from society would prevent them inflicting damage on others. However, it is clear that he felt a moral dilemma with his solution to the problem. He was aware that it was a gross infringement to the civil liberties of an individual to lock them away purely because of their low intellect, but he argued that:

> 'it cannot be too strongly impressed upon our notice that every imbecile, especially the high-grade imbecile, is a

63

potential criminal, needing only the proper environment and opportunities for the development and expression of his criminal tendencies.'

Auden's view was equally shared by Charles Buckman Goring (1870-1919), who was employed as a medical officer at Broadmoor. Goring undertook a comprehensive work entitled *The English convict: a statistical study,* published in 1913 when he was Deputy Medical Officer at HM Prison, Parkhurst, which set out to establish whether there were any significant physical or mental abnormalities among the criminal classes that set them apart from ordinary men. His crusade against crime came to the conclusion that:

'To modify inherited tendency by appropriate educational measures; or else to modify opportunity for crime by segregation and supervision of the unfit; or else – and this is attacking the evil at its very roots – to regulate the reproduction of those degrees of constitutional qualities – feeblemindedness, inebriety, epilepsy, deficient social instinct, etc – which conduce to the committing of crime.'

Goring was not alone in this belief – Mary Dendy, a campaigner for reform from North Wales, was also firmly of the opinion that segregation from society and strict birth control of those deemed to be feeble-minded was a necessity in conquering crime as these individuals could mask their low intellect and have a negative influence on other children. She was of the belief that people with learning disabilities should be kept in special residential schools and helped establish a colony for the feeble-minded in Manchester which opened as the Sandlebridge Colony in Cheshire in 1902. Mary Dendy was a member of the Eugenics Education Society who argued 'for the good of the race the mentally subnormal should be prevented from breeding'.

Crime caused as a result of an excess of alcohol was also reaching epidemic proportions, and despite the best endeavours of the Temperance Society in attempting to curb the problems of drunkenness, it continued to escalate in the nineteenth century. Many individuals became notorious due to their drunken behaviour, and the press eagerly reported cases, particularly if they involved inebriated women.

As the streets began to fill with drunkards and prisons and asylums admitted more and more people with alcohol related problems, a group of doctors lobbied parliament requesting legislation so that they could treat drunkenness as a disease. The Inebriates Acts of 1879 and 1898 were the result of these endeavours and provided a convenient political solution to the perceived moral and physical disaster of intemperance affecting men and women of all social classes, but increasingly and without doubt most visibly, among the 'lower classes'. The new Acts allowed for the establishment of private inebriate retreats or colonies for wealthy people and state run inebriate reformatories for criminal drunkards. Described in some newspapers as 'The Drunkards' Bill', the Acts provided the licensing of 'retreats' where individuals could be detained at their own request or the request of parents, spouse or guardian for a period of not less than one month but not exceeding a year. Habitual drunkards were defined as 'people who by reason of habitual intemperance are dangerous to himself or to others or incapable of managing their affairs'. Magistrates also had the power to admit those who had been convicted of being drunk and disorderly in three consecutive months.

In much the same way that asylums had been funded and provided at county level following lunacy legislation at the beginning of the nineteenth century, inebriate reformatories began to spring up around the country from the 1870s onwards. By the 1890s, the Home Secretary had appointed a Departmental Committee to consider and advise on the regulations and recommendations which should be made respecting these reformatories and changed the length of admission to three years if necessary. Committee members included Dr H.B Donkin, a Commissioner of Prisons, and Dr Richard Brayn, the Medical Superintendent of Broadmoor.

Philanthropists also set up their own inebriate colonies to assist – mainly women drunkards – the growing dependence on alcohol. One such person was Lady Isabella Somerset. Lady Isabella became interested in the temperance movement after a close friend committed suicide while intoxicated. Eloquent, compelling and an heiress in her own right, she was elected president of the British Women's Temperance Association in 1890. The Association established a Colony for Women Inebriates, in Surrey in 1895. This facility was intended to rehabilitate female alcoholics of all classes. A 180-acre estate at Duxhurst, just outside Reigate, was chosen as the site for the home. It contained a manor house, a farm and its own infirmary and church so was perfect for recovery and rehabilitation. The estate was secured on a long lease by the British Women's Temperance Association and the Industrial Farm Colony was formally opened on 6 July 1896 by Princess Mary, Duchess of Teck. It had accommodation for 40 patients, who were expected to stay at least one year.

All classes of inebriates were accepted, but they were housed separately. The Manor House, known as the Sanatorium, had been built as a gentleman's residence and was surrounded by extensive gardens and grounds. This provided accommodation for higher class ladies and stage celebrities suffering from alcoholism and weekly charges were between two and five guineas.

A second class of provision was situated about a mile away from the Manor House. Known as Hope House, it received middle-class women who paid up to 30 shillings a week. A third home admitted poor and destitute inebriates of the working classes. These patients lived in single-storey purpose-built thatched cottages (six of which had been built by 1896), arranged around three sides of a village green.

Keeping the women busy was considered to be an important part of the rehabilitation process, and they were taught skills which would be useful to them after they left the Colony, including weaving, basket-making and pottery. Other domestic duties included knitting, sewing and embroidery. Patients were paid for their employment and once the weekly charges for their keep had been deducted, the remainder was held in safe-keeping for them until they were discharged.

Lady Isabella lived on the estate and devoted herself to the Colony, working with the patients and usually wearing a nurse's uniform. Following the 1898 Inebriates Act, the Colony became licensed to receive twelve inebriates usually from the 'lower class' who were sent by the courts as an alternative to prison.

In 1899, after four years of operation, of the 112 women who had been discharged, 55 were reported to be doing well. In 1902, the Medical Officer for the Colony claimed a 45 per cent success rate in the cure from alcoholism.

One case which was not a success was that of Jane Cakebread, described as 'the most drunken woman in Britain'. Lady Isabella made many attempts to help her but alcohol was too ingrained in her psyche.

Jane Cakebread

Jane was born in Sawbridgeworth, Hertfordshire in 1835 but moved to London as a young girl to take up a position as a domestic servant. In her twenties she was a housemaid in the home of Charles Hardy who was a member of the London Stock Exchange. Jane never married, but during her youth had courted a doctor who wished to marry her. It is possible that he changed his mind when she began to drink because Jane remained a spinster for life. She attempted to reform, signing the pledge at a coffee stall at Stamford Hill following an early release from Holloway Prison on a charge of drunkenness.

On 26 January 1884, she was charged at Clerkenwell Police Court for committing malicious damage after breaking a pane of glass when drunk and 50 other convictions for drunkenness. Found guilty of wilful damage, she was sentenced to 12 calendar months in Millbank Prison. Jane's infamy as 'a champion drunkard' was devoured by the press from this point on. Her court appearances were regularly reported and her continual assurances that she would 'take the pledge' amused the court gallery of spectators.

In 1895 Lady Isabella Somerset offered Jane a place at the newly opened Colony for Women Inebriates, which she refused. She was interviewed by the *London Daily Chronicle* who were intrigued to discover why she had turned down such a generous offer. Jane replied:

> 'The're kind to me at 'Olloway, especially this time, for I was in hospital and got a chop – which was not strange to me as a lady – and I 'ad no work to do, though I'm clean and the best needlewoman in 'Olloway, as they will tell you. They knows me best there. What is to happen to me now I've left 'Olloway? Are we not told, 'Boast not thus of the morrow for thou knowest not what a day may bring forth'. I mean no offence but I'm goin' to no 'ome – not I, at present anyhow. Oh, it's not an 'ome at all they says, and I'll just do what I likes, and perhaps that's so – but I'm goin' to my own friends, I am.'

Jane returned to her friends arriving at Sawbridgeworth near Bishops Stortford having travelled from Liverpool Street Station. At Sawbridgeworth, she visited her brother, but by evening all her good intentions had disappeared and she was apprehended for being drunk and disorderly and using obscene language and was up before the magistrate the next morning. She was sentenced to one month hard labour in Cambridge Gaol.

During this incarceration, she made the decision to change her life and asked the chaplain to assist her in obtaining the place in Surrey previously offered by Lady Isabella Somerset. Convinced of her desire to become teetotal, the chaplain paid her fare to South Tottenham so that she might consult Mr Holmes, a police court missionary. Mr Holmes was also convinced of her sincerity and later described her as:

> 'not a drunkard, not a dipsomaniac in the ordinary sense. The effect of the drink upon her is mental, not physical – a mental excitement. She has rarely been convicted for being drunk and incapable, it is always drunk and disorderly.'

Mr Holmes accompanied Jane to the cottage provided by Lady Isabella – which was four miles from the nearest public house, and she shed tears of contentment when she took possession of her new home hoping to spend the rest of her days in law abiding peace.

Unfortunately, Jane's stay in Surrey did not last long. She gave so much trouble that it proved impossible to keep her and during a church service she sprang from the pew and shouted in a loud voice, 'I am Jane Cakebread!' A medical man was consulted to determine her mental state and he certified her insane. Lady Isabella declared that she was not an inebriate as she had not had any drink while in Reigate nor had shown any craving for it. Without doubt she was insane and the smallest amount of alcohol rendered her a dangerous lunatic. Her proper place should be in a workhouse asylum not in a prison cell.

In January 1896, Jane was before the North London Police Court once again on a charge of drunkenness. She told the magistrate that she had been treated like a lady while in Reigate, but she had not been comfortable as the other women there were not to her taste. During her stay she had hemmed 120 towels, 18 table-cloths and a number of articles of children's clothing. Lady Isabella had given her a nice dress and a beautiful Bible. The police court missionary, Mr Holmes, stated that without doubt she was not in her right mind, commenting that she had a delusion that she was entitled to receive a fortune of £17,000. Jane Cakebread disagreed with their conclusions and categorically stated that she would not go to the workhouse but would happily go back to Holloway Prison. Her request was granted – for one week while her sanity was examined.

Jane was sent to Claybury Lunatic Asylum at Woodford Bridge in Essex, where she believed that she had been sent to protect the other inmates. Within two years of her admission she began to fail and Mr Holmes visited her but she failed to recognise him. She died on 3 December 1898.

Following her death, Dr Robert Jones, medical superintendent of Claybury Asylum, wrote an article on her psychology which was published in the *British Medical Journal* in 1904. His article made it clear that Jane Cakebread had intrigued the public for many years. She was the subject of many inches of newspaper coverage as her drunken antics were described in great detail much to the delight of the readers.

Ellen Sweeney

Ellen Sweeney was born in Swansea in about 1840 and was referred to in the press as the 'Welsh Jane Cakebread'. Described as 'notorious', 'a social pest' and an 'incorrigible drunkard', she was first convicted before the age of 20 and spent more than half her life in Swansea Gaol charged with being drunk and disorderly.

In 1874, she created such a drunken disturbance in the Crown public house in Swansea that she had to be taken to the police station on a stretcher. It was widely believed in the area that Ellen was not able to control herself, and that her brain was affected due to drink. Despite this, she continued on her road to self-destruction and was homeless and desolate. Her dependence on alcohol weakened her and after only one glass she would either break windows or sit down on doorsteps and make hideous noises.

Towards the end of her life, the local magistrates wisely kept her as a permanent inmate of Swansea workhouse, where she passed away on 20 August 1896 due to enlargement of the liver. Described by the local press as a 'very emaciated and weakly-looking woman, without a tooth in her head', Ellen was not an immoral character and drunkenness and disorderly conduct were practically her only offences. Although only 56 years old when she died, she had notched up 280 convictions for drunkenness during her lifetime.

The few assets that she had were left to a local undertaker to ensure that she received a proper burial. She was buried in Danygraig Cemetery in Swansea. The town mourned 'Poor Ellen', and the newspapers missed reporting her many exploits. *The Cambrian* blamed society rather than Ellen for the situation she found herself in commenting that inebriates should not spend their lives between the gaol and the workhouse as they were not responsible for their actions. The Inebriate Act aimed to help individuals such as Ellen who through circumstances beyond their control found themselves in a cycle of alcoholic excess and gaol admission.

A Home Office circular of 1889 instructed magistrates to dismiss the less serious cases that came before them if they involved a weak-minded offender and that these individuals should either be placed in the guardianship of friends or sent to an asylum. This would prevent prisons from filling up with offenders with mental health disorders and allow them to be incarcerated in a place where their difficulties were understood.

However, not all in the legal profession agreed with this apparent lax attitude. In 1905, Sir Edward Fry, late Lord Justice of Appeal, advocated an iron-handed method of dealing with the habitual criminal. When giving evidence before the Royal Commission on the Care of the Feeble-Minded he stated:

> 'I have a strong and increasing impression that the Law ought to allow the absolute segregation or imprisonment for life of persons who will go on committing crimes. My view may be wrong, but it is that one of the rights of the State to inflict punishment for the protection of society from the depredations of a certain class of persons, whether imbecile or not imbecile. The State ought to have the right to imprison a person for life whenever the evidence goes to show that he is an habitual criminal, who, directly he comes out of prison, is committing crime again.'

Chapter 8

Poverty, infirmity and illegitimacy

During the nineteenth century, children were strongly dependent on the presence of both parents within the family home. With the father as the breadwinner, often working long hours, it was the responsibility of the mother to care for the children and organise household affairs. Many families suffered if either parent was unable to fulfil these roles. On occasion, this led to some sad cases of child murder due to extreme poverty, disability or illegitimacy.

When families had no prospect of a living wage due to a lack of employment, sickness or disability, their only hope was the assistance of other family members. If this was not available, then an application to the Parish for poor relief would be attempted or as a last resort, they would be admitted to the workhouse. The Poor Law Amendment Act had been introduced in 1834 in England and Wales (a similar Act for Scotland was passed in 1845) in an attempt to reduce the cost of looking after the poor by ensuring that they would be housed in workhouses. It also curbed the abuse of the system by the 'idle poor' who claimed relief in preference to working. A key proposal of the Poor Law Act was that 'except as to medical attendance ... all relief whatever to able-bodied persons or to their families, otherwise than in well-regulated workhouses ... shall be declared unlawful and shall cease'.

The workhouse would therefore be the sole form of relief for many paupers in Victorian Britain. One Assistant Commissioner was quoted as believing:

> 'new life, new energy, is infused into the constitution of the pauper; he is aroused like one from sleep. He surveys his former employers with new eyes. He begs a job – he will not take a denial – he discovers that everyone wants something to be done. He desires to make up this man's hedges, to clear out another man's ditches, to grub stumps out of hedgerows for a third. He is ready to turn his hand to anything.'

Poor Law Commissioners realised that the housing conditions of many paupers were so inadequate that anything would seem luxurious in comparison. Despite there being less eligibility under the terms of the new Acts, to prevent a huge influx into workhouses and ensuring they were places of last resort, conditions were such as to make the experience as unappealing as possible. People would be clothed and fed in return for several hours work each day, but families would be separated, divided by gender. These establishments became feared as 'prisons for the poor'. Many people would do all they could to prevent being admitted.

Without doubt, the fear of poverty and an admission to the workhouse would have played on the minds of many of the poorer classes of society. Already struggling with daily life in inadequate living conditions and frequently with many children, some of whom would not survive infancy, those already predisposed to melancholia could become increasingly despondent, dispirited and downcast and descend into more extreme forms of mental health problems.

Sarah Dickinson (or Dickenson)

In March 1844, Sarah Dickinson, a 36-year-old wife and mother from Giffin Street, Deptford stood trial at the Old Bailey on a charge of multiple murder. She and her husband, John Fawley Dickinson, lived in very distressed circumstances as he had been out of work for nearly two years due to ill health. The family took lodgers into their home and also received a small amount of money from family. However, this was insufficient to feed, clothe and house them adequately. In order to obtain food for their two children, George John, 3-years-old, and Jane Eliza, 20-months, they pawned their belongings, keeping only enough clothing to keep them clean. Anxious to conceal their extreme poverty, they were reluctant to seek assistance from the parish relieving officer in case they were admitted to the local workhouse, where the family would have been separated.

They continued like this for many months until Sarah became unwell from malnourishment. She fed her children before herself but they rarely had more than a little bread and butter each day. Sarah began to complain about pains in her head and expressed a concern that she should lose her senses. Her neighbours stated it was clear that her mind was wandering.

On the morning of 10 January 1844, Sarah's husband left the house early in an attempt to find work for the day. When he returned home in the evening he found that his two children were dead with their throats cut and his wife was bleeding profusely from a neck wound. A surgeon managed to save Sarah's life but it was thought very likely that she would die as she had severed her windpipe.

At her trial, several witnesses gave evidence that Sarah suffered bouts of mental ill-health and complained frequently of pains in her head. Her brother-in-law gave evidence that shortly before her marriage in 1839 she had fallen downstairs, hitting her head after which she was unwell for several months. It transpired during the trial that there was a history of insanity in Sarah's family – a sister, Maria March, was confined in an asylum considered incurable.

On the evidence of medical experts, Sarah was deemed unaccountable for her actions when she murdered her children and was found not guilty, being at the time in a state of insanity. Sarah was admitted to Bethlehem from Newgate Prison following her trial and attempted to commit suicide on several occasions. She remained there for the next ten years before being transferred to Fisherton House Asylum in February 1854 – a move she objected to but could do nothing to prevent

On 2 December 1854, she was pardoned for her crime and released. Her husband John died shortly after her trial in 1844.

Mary Ann Hamilton

The Hamilton family also lived in extreme poverty off Oxford Street in London. Joseph and Mary Ann Hamilton had two small children – three-year-old Ellen, who was paralysed down one side of her body, and 11-month-old Henry. Ellen suffered from frequent epileptic seizures and was regularly very unwell. Her father, a tailor, had been in and out of work for at least two years as a consequence of his daughter's disability. As a result, both parents were in a bad state of health and poverty as Joseph often earned nothing for weeks.

On 15 December 1861, Mary Ann approached Police Sergeant George Brown and enquired the way to Brook Green Station as she wished to give herself up for the murder of one of her children. He asked her why she had committed such a crime. She replied, 'for want; I could not see it want for bread any longer.' Sergeant Brown took Mary Ann into custody and then proceeded to her home address at 9 Rebecca Court, Wells Street, which he described as:

> 'a poor, miserable place; the worst place I was ever in, for a dwelling, there was not a bit of anything in the shape of food, it exhibited every sign of great want, in every way – the whole of the bed clothing to the bed was an old, dirty, calico sheet.'

In this 'home' he found two children lying on an old flock bed – the little girl was alive and paralysed down one side but the younger child was lying on the farther side of the bed with a piece of braid tied tightly around his neck. Wrapping the body of the dead boy in the bed sheet the police officer took both children to the workhouse. Mary Ann was concerned that her little girl was still alive saying, 'I could not hurt her as she is paralysed' and that she was sorry that she had killed her son.

Mary Ann Hamilton was tried at the Old Bailey in January 1862 and found not guilty on the grounds of insanity. She was ordered to be detained until Her Majesty's pleasure be known. Mary Ann was one of the first patients to be transferred from Bethlehem to Broadmoor where she died on 8 January 1910 aged 85 from senile decay.

Mary Ann's husband, Joseph, died in 1868 after which their daughter, Ellen, who repeatedly asked for her mother, was admitted as a patient to the asylum at Hampstead. She was transferred to the Metropolitan District Asylum for Idiots in Lower Clapton on 3 May 1875 and died there on 21 December 1875 from consumption with atrophy of the left side of the brain.

Ann Randle

On 8 October 1887, Ann Randle took two rooms on the first floor of 11, Lower Road, Richmond, Surrey at a rent of a guinea and a half a week to board her and her four children. The property, which was a coffee shop, belonged to John William Benbow and his wife Sarah. On 28 October, Ann rented a third room at an additional one shilling a week for the use of a nurse, Ethel Tritton.

Ann was known to her landlord and to her nurse as Mrs Wesley, the wife of a commercial traveller. She had two sons, Samuel and Harold who were six and five-years-old respectively, and two daughters, Mary and Dorothy. Ann came from a reasonably wealthy background. Her father, Simeon Eveleigh, was steward to Lord Bolingbroke and she had been born and brought up in Lydiard Tregoze, Wiltshire. It is unlikely that she had ever experienced any real financial hardship. However, poverty is relative and following the premature death of her husband, Samuel Beavis Randle, on 29 November 1884 after only three years marriage she doubtless felt herself to be in a vulnerable position. Samuel Randle had been a boarding house proprietor in Bournemouth. When he died at the age of 42 years, he left an estate valued at less than £100 for the maintenance of his widow Ann and their three children, Samuel, Mary and Harold all of whom were under three years of age.

Following the death of her husband, Ann appears to have had a relationship with a Mr Wesley and used his name although the couple were not married. She had a daughter, Dorothy Wesley Randle, in London in 1886. A year later, Ann was on her own with all four children. The nurse that she hired to help look after them had never met Mr Wesley.

By December 1886, Ann was in arrears with her rent to the sum of £21 and her landlady, Mrs Benbow, began to press her for the money. The nurse was also due payment but accepted a ring from Ann instead of her salary. On the evening of Sunday 4 December, Mrs Benbow informed Ann that she would have to leave the premises the following morning as she could no longer afford to keep her without rental payment.

Ann, desperate with her situation and with nowhere else to go, gave each of her four children a spoonful of laudanum which she had been prescribed as an external treatment for neuralgia and drank the rest of the bottle herself. The following morning, nurse Ethel Tritton, was unable to wake Ann and discovered that although the children were slightly drowsy, they appeared well although Harold and Mary had been sick in the night. Alerting Mrs Benbow to the situation, Ann's surgeon, Dr Herbert Frederick Chapman, was called to tend to the family. He determined that the children were unharmed, but Ann was in too much of a stupor to be roused. Ann had written a note confessing that she had poisoned herself and her children. As a result, the police also arrived at the property.

> 'In the event of my death I have tonight taken some laudanum, and given some to each of my darlings I could not leave them to face this cold world alone; they will be better off while as for me I have been driven mad by one thing and another. God forgive me having been left alone to fight and struggle, and life has become a burden to me. Make no inquiries about me,

but will some friend who has cared for me see me buried with my little dear ones. I am so tired, heart sick, and will some kind friend see any money owing to me to the people here paid. I have given to Ethel my nurse, a ring to sell; she is also to have my clothes. Mr. Wesley knows about the thing in the Tottenham Court Road, and he can do as he thinks best.'

Police Inspector James Aldridge accompanied by Sergeant George Bush, arrested her for poisoning her four children, and also for taking poison herself. Ann commented:

'What with one thing and the other, and Mrs. Benbow worrying me, I don't know what I did do, and I would do away with the children even now, and if you do not take me away I will strangle myself, or bite the vein in my arm and bleed to death.'

The police, informing her that she would be taken to an institution where she would be cared for until she recovered, took her to the Richmond Union Infirmary. Her four children were taken to the local workhouse. On 8 December 1887, Ann was moved to Holloway Gaol to await trial.

Ann was tried on 27 February 1888 at the Old Bailey for feloniously 'administering a quantity of aconite to Samuel Everleigh Randle with intent to murder' and with attempting to commit suicide. She was charged on a second count with also 'administering laudanum with like intent'. The case was heard before Henry Hawkins, 1st Baron Brampton (1817-1907). Her surgeon, Dr Chapman gave evidence that she was suffering from mental depression with suicidal tendencies and she ought to have been kept under supervision. Ann herself made a statement which said, 'I think I had better say nothing; my head is not every clear, and I may say what is incorrect.' She was found not guilty and discharged.

Harold was sent to a children's home in Leyton which was chargeable under Bethnal Green poor rates. As he was not from the parish, the authorities went to considerable trouble to determine his parentage and place of birth so that they would not be financially responsible for him. Failing to find his mother and discovering that his father had died, they removed him to Islington where he had been born. He joined the King's Royal Rifles as a private in 1901 and after 12 years' service in the British Army, he joined the Royal North West Mounted Police Division of the Canadian Overseas Expeditionary Force.

Ann's other children were reunited with her, and following her marriage in 1895, to William Thomas Wood, an Irish violinist, she went on to have three more sons. Twins, William and Thomas were born in 1896 and Charles two years later.

Louisa Cameron

Louisa Boyd was born on 5 July 1860 in Toxteth Park, Liverpool, daughter of Robert Boyd, a shipwright and his wife Mary Jane. On 7 April 1877, aged 17 years, she married George Lewis Cameron at All Soul's Church, Liverpool. The couple had nine children – eight sons, and one daughter, Matilda, born between 1878 and 1898, – but three of their sons died in infancy.

By 1903, two sons had left home to join the armed forces – Ainger was a gunner in the Royal Garrison Artillery and George had joined the Royal Navy as a Boy 2nd Class. In 1907, Louisa and her husband George were living in Vaughan Street, Toxteth Park, Liverpool with their four remaining children. Their youngest child was nine-year-old Charles who had learning difficulties and had spent time at St Vincent's Orphanage for Roman Catholic Boys in Beacon Lane, Everton, Liverpool.

Louisa had begun to suffer from a nervous debility, and by April 1907 after complaining of pains in her head, was seen by a doctor. Her husband was away from home looking for work and her daughter Matilda had been accused of stealing a sovereign. As her children sat quarrelling and making fun of her youngest son Charles, Louisa told them 'you will not long have him to hit. I will get rid of him before I get rid of myself'. Clearly feeling stressed by the situation she found herself in, things became worse when on 9 April 1907, she received a letter from her son George aboard HMS Triumph.

> 'Dear Mother,
> I am sorry to say I can't see you before my twentieth birthday, and when I do see you I will have a good reckoning with you. When I come to look over my correspondence with you it makes my whole frame shake to think I have not got a better home to go to.'

Later the same afternoon, Louisa's youngest son Charles returned home from school and asked her for some food. Without warning, Louisa took the kitchen knife and cut his throat killing him instantly. Realising what she had done, she stood at her front doorstep holding out her blood-stained hands, pleading with passers-by to let her die. When she was arrested for the murder, she cried, 'Oh my child what have I done, I have been low spirited lately. Poverty has done this'.

Taken to Walton Gaol to await trial, Louisa was assessed by the prison doctor. She expressed concern about what would have happened to her young son if she had died and believed it was in his best interests that he should die before her. The doctor was of the opinion that she was suffering from melancholia and was both suicidal and homicidal. Louisa stood trial at Liverpool Assizes on 9 May 1907 before William Pickford, 1st Baron Sterndale (1848-1923). She was found guilty but insane and ordered to be detained until His Majesty's pleasure be known. On 16 May 1907 Louisa was admitted to Broadmoor for an indefinite period.

Illegitimacy by the nineteenth century was considered to be a moral issue and one which should be discouraged in an effort to restore female morality. The Commission of Inquiry looking at the Poor Law placed two Bastardy Clauses at the end of their Report. Its results revealed that the Poor Law which had been enacted in 1733, encouraged licentiousness and illegitimacy because parish relief was readily available for women and their illegitimate offspring.

The Poor Law Amendment Act of 1834 attempted to restore virtue to the lower classes of society by removing Bastardy Clauses from the old Poor Law which made men responsible for the maintenance of their children – legitimate or not. Under the old system, men who refused to support their children could be arrested and imprisoned and the mother and children would be cared for from public funds which the father would have to reimburse. Removing this clause in 1834, absolved fathers of any responsibility for their bastard children and as a result, women were economically victimised by society. Mothers of illegitimate children were treated in the same way as widows for poor relief – they were expected to support themselves and their offspring. Many were unable to do so ensuring that children were brought up in poverty. Malnutrition was rife, and the mental well-being of single mothers suffered. With few options available, many mothers either entered the workhouse or handed their children to unscrupulous baby farmers. A report in *The Cambrian* newspaper dated 30 January 1836 attempted to highlight the problems of the new system:

> 'Whatever difference of opinion may exist as to the other provisions of the New Poor Law, both its advocates and opponents

are, we believe, very fast falling into an entire coincidence as to the injustice, the cruelty and impolicy of the clauses regarding illegitimate children. Under this head the worst prognostics of the opponents of the measure are every day being fulfilled to the letter, while parishes, which were to have been benefited by the measure, are, next to mothers and helpless infants, the greatest sufferers by it being in most cases left without any remedy at all. That abortion, child-murder, and desertion, are among its consequences, now admits of no doubt.'

The sad case of a young mother with two illegitimate children and a third on the way highlights the difficulties faced by many women unfortunate enough not to have the support of a husband. For some, it was preferable to kill their children and commit suicide than continue with the situation they found themselves in.

Ann Dickinson

Twenty-four-year old Ann Dickinson lived on the outskirts of Greetland, a small village three miles from Halifax in West Yorkshire. Her parents had kept the Rose and Crown Inn in the village, but both had died. Ann lived alone with her two young children, Arthur, aged three, and Gertrude, aged 14 months. She made a living by taking in washing and as a charwoman for other households in the district.

The father of her children, Fred Heys, a cloth presser also from Greetland, gave Ann £25 following the birth of her first child, and also provided her with a weekly allowance of five shillings and sixpence for both children. Although the couple were unmarried, Fred continued to spend most evenings in Ann's home. In 1897, Ann discovered that she was pregnant for a third time and informed Fred that he was about to become a father yet again. However, Fred refused to accept responsibility for the new baby, claiming that she had other gentlemen visitors. Ann vowed to drown herself as a result of the situation she found herself in.

In the early hours of Friday 20 August 1897, Ann went into labour. Tying Gertrude in a linen sling around her waist she made for Clay House Mill Dam about 400 yards from her cottage. Plunging into the water, she discovered that the dam was not deep enough and scrambled out again. Unfortunately, Gertrude was not so lucky and as she entered the water the linen sling gave way and she drowned. Returning home in an advanced state of labour, Ann gave birth to a little boy, Thomas. Her neighbour, Ann Schofield heard her cries and finding the door open, entered the cottage. Discovering that Ann was wet she asked her what had occurred and was told, 'I have drowned my baby and tried to drown myself, fetch the police.' Police Constable Hart arrived to discover Ann upstairs on the bed with her new baby saying she wished she was dead. Her boots were discovered by the mill dam along with a letter addressed to Fred Heys. Ann was taken to Halifax Workhouse Infirmary. A post mortem examination of Gertrude revealed that she had died of drowning, and although 14 months old, she weighed only eight pounds – the same as her newborn brother.

Eliza Ann Helliwell, wife of Robinson Helliwell, a weaver from Cunny Lane, Greetland gave evidence at the subsequent inquest. She stated that she had been present when Gertrude was born and the little girl had been healthy and of average size at birth but had become emaciated since. Ann had been in low spirits for some time due to her pregnancy and inadequate food. Eliza Ann had frequently taken food to the cottage for the children as she believed the family were hungry although Ann had never complained.

Fred Heys was also questioned at the inquest and Ann's letter to him read out for the jury's benefit. The letter stated that she was going to drown herself as she could not exist with three children, as she had found it hard to struggle with two and had lived a life of misery:

> 'You have behaved to me shamefully, and then for you to say that this child is not yours. I can say with all consciousness that all the three are yours. You told me on Saturday night that I did not know who was the father of the first. I can stand it no longer. I will take the child and I want you to look after little Arthur for my sake. I could go better if it was not for leaving him. You have ruined me, and if you only would have got married it would have saved all this. Good bye to all my brothers and sisters.'

The jury returned a verdict of wilful murder against Ann, but they were unanimously of the opinion that she had been driven by despair to commit the deed. Ann was tried at Leeds Assizes in the autumn of 1897 and ordered to be detained during Her Majesty's pleasure but was given a conditional pardon by the Home Secretary in 1899.

She was homed with the Sisters at Horbury House of Mercy near Wakefield, Yorkshire where she became a kitchen maid. This establishment was an Anglican religious order of Augustinians founded in England in 1852 by Harriet Monsell, who was the first Superior, and Thomas Thellusson Carter, a priest at Windsor. The purpose of the order was to help marginalised women, mainly single mothers, the homeless and prostitutes by providing them shelter and teaching them a trade. The work of the sisters expanded to include administering and working in orphanages, schools, convalescent hospitals, soup kitchens, and women's hostels.

As his mother requested, Arthur Dickinson was brought up by his father, remaining with him after Fred's marriage to Mary Ann Bennett on 7 March 1903 in Walsden, St Peter, Yorkshire. Fred died in 1918 aged 48. Thomas Dickinson, the baby born to Ann after she tried to kill herself, died in 1898 aged 14 months.

A sad Scottish case highlights the problems many people had when disability affected someone within the family. Unlike the cases examined earlier in this chapter, Helen M'Kinnis was not a child – but she had a disability that required her to be cared for as she would struggle to live on her own. Having received the assistance of institutional teaching until she was 14, there was little provision for her welfare beyond this age apart from the loving kindness of her family. This left her in a very vulnerable position.

Thomas M'Kinnis

In 1839, 30-year-old Thomas M'Kinnis and his 24-year-old sister, Helen, lived together in King Street, Glasgow. Helen was both deaf and dumb and in 1823, when she was eight years old, she became a pupil at the Glasgow Deaf and Dumb Institution which had been founded in 1819. The Institution only took pupils between the ages of seven and fourteen years, so Helen was obliged to leave and return to her family in 1830. She moved to live with her brother Thomas, who was a bootmaker.

Helen M'Kinnis visited the Institution in January 1839, to ask for their assistance in finding her work, and arrangements were made for her to start employment in a warehouse in Glasgow the following week. Tragically, Helen did not live long enough to take up the job. Her brother had for several years been concerned that Helen would die of starvation and had made several attempts to gain assistance to ensure that this would not happen – all without success. Certain that she was miserable and in order to put an end to her supposed suffering he made the decision that she would be better off dead.

On Saturday 12 January 1839, he waited until she was asleep before lighting a candle to see which way she was lying in her bed. Extinguishing the light as he did not want her to see him committing murder, he prodded her with a knife as he was uncertain how to kill somebody, never having done it before. Startled, Helen woke up and grabbed him by the neck after which Thomas stabbed her 13 times and saw her fall over a tub, dead. In Thomas' mind he still needed to care for her, so he laid her out and covered her with a sheet. Changing his bloodied shirt, he went to friends in the Saltmarket. Due to his incoherent ramblings, they felt he may have assaulted his sister.

The police were called and Captain Miller of the Glasgow Constabulary took Thomas into custody. Thomas explained that he loved Helen but 'afraid that she might come to want and misery – all that I have done was for her good' he resolved to save her from her misery by 'putting her out of the world'. He was seen to be experiencing serious hallucinations and when he saw his reflection in a mirror on the police office wall he started shaking, went pale and almost collapsed, shouting 'Oh God, oh God!' The police superintendent obtained a latch-key to the house in King Street to see if Thomas' story was true. There he found Helen's naked dead body lying on the floor, drenched in blood and covered with wounds.

After he was examined, the police asked Thomas whether he would prefer to be sent to the jail or the bridewell. He seemed outraged and speaking incoherently stated that he had done nothing wrong, having done the community a great service which entitled him to their applause. The law had not provided for his sister, so he had taken matters into his own hands and should be congratulated. There seemed little doubt regarding his sanity and a search of his home discovered large amounts of writing in which Thomas described that 'he walked in glory with the pretty 'gairls' and descends from his paradise to describe the movement of a fly on the wall, or the flight of a crow in the air'.

Thomas was tried at the Circuit Court of Glasgow on 6 May 1839 before Alexander Maconochie, Lord Meadowbank. He was found to be insane and therefore 'not an object of punishment'. He was ordered to be 'imprisoned in the Bridewell of Glasgow for life, or until caution or surety is found by his friends to the extent of £100 sterling for his safe keeping in custody all the days of his life'. When the sentence was read, Thomas made a speech declaring that although he was an injured man he was the 'Great Lord of All'.

On 13 November 1840, after six months in the Glasgow Bridewell, he was admitted to the Royal Lunatic Asylum, Dundee, and subsequently transferred to the Criminal Lunatic Department at Perth on 4 May 1847. He died there on 11 September 1873 from cirrhosis of the liver, aged 64 years.

Chapter 9

Children who kill

Murders by children were unusual but not unheard of in Victorian Britain. The judicial system was inconsistent in dealing with their offences, and newspapers sensationalised crimes providing the public with lurid details of the murders. Mental health disorders were increasingly recognised, and provision was developed for children within the asylum system. In the early part of Queen Victoria's reign there remained little sympathy for children who killed and the consequences it had on their families.

William Newton Allnutt

Samuel Nelme, of Grove Place, Hackney in London was a gentleman of 'fortune and respectability' – a man of independent means who had been married twice. A daughter from his first marriage, Mary Louisa, married Thomas Alexander Allnutt on 6 November 1832 in St John, Hackney. The couple had eleven children, three of whom died in infancy. Their third child, William Newton Allnutt was born on 7 October 1835 in Sutton Courtenay, Berkshire. When William was 18 months old, he was injured by a plough which caused considerable damage to his head and it was believed he would die. William survived this accident, but his behaviour became difficult – he heard voices in his head, walked in his sleep and his mother struggled with his behaviour which she declared was different from her other children:

> 'I have had a good deal of trouble with him, and have on several occasions been obliged to remonstrate with him—I have children older than him, and know the general disposition of children.'

In April 1845, the family travelled to Hastings to take the sea air. Mary Louisa was expecting another child who would be born and die shortly after their arrival, and her husband was suffering from mental health problems. He died later the same year, after which Mary Louisa and 11-year-old William moved to London to live with her father and his second wife Sarah. Despite the difficulties she had with her third son, she kept him close to her, although her five eldest children were sent away to school and the youngest two were boarded with friends in the country. Mary Louisa stated in court that her deceased husband had died in a state of complete madness. He was 'a person of an extremely excitable habit and mind' who had been in the habit of drinking and also suffered from epileptic attacks which made him exceedingly violent. Thomas' father was subject to paralysis and his two sisters were blind 'from a nervous disease, called amaurosis'.

Therefore, Mary, recently widowed and having just lost her newborn daughter, Victoria Adelaide, moved to Grove Place, Hackney with her son William where her father kept a quantity of arsenic in a locked bureau to kill rats. William became intrigued with the poison and a week before his grandfather died, he asked his mother what it was like. She told him that it was like flour.

Shortly afterwards, William's grandfather became ill and his mother and grandmother also felt decidedly unwell. Despite the ministrations of doctors on 27 October 1847, Samuel Nelme died after suffering from extreme stomach pains and vomiting for several days. Initially it was suspected he had cholera, known as 'the poisoner's friend' as the symptoms were much the same. However, following a post mortem it was discovered that there was a quantity of arsenic in his body which he had inadvertently administered from a sugar basin which was used to accompany fruit.

While the coroner for East Middlesex, William Baker, opened an inquest into the death of Samuel, William Allnutt, who was to be provided for in his grandfather's will, was in Worship Street Police Office charged with having stolen a gold watch and other articles of jewellery worth 70 guineas from his grandmother. He confessed to his mother and begged forgiveness for the crime stating that a voice appeared to tell him, 'Do it, do it, you will not be found out.' The items were retrieved from the gutter of an adjoining house where he had thrown them, as was a pistol, the purchase of which was traced back to William.

While in jail he attended worship and after listening to a sermon which advocated the confession of sins to absolve guilt he wrote a letter to his mother asking for forgiveness for poisoning his grandfather. The letter was produced at his Old Bailey trial, and the jury heard that William had placed arsenic in the sugar bowl to injure his grandfather following an altercation with him the previous week. He had taken a beating and was knocked down in the hallway:

> 'On the 20th of Oct. grandfather went to his desk for the key of the wine-cellar to get some wine up and to look over his accounts; and whilst he was gone I took the poison out, and emptied some of it into another piece of paper, and put the other back; and then after dinner I put it in the sugar-basin; and why I did it was I had made grandfather angry with something I had done, and he knocked me down in the passage, and my head went up against the table and hurt it very much, and he said next time I did it, he would almost kill me; but in future I will say the truth and nothing but the truth: as grandfather said, "Truth may be blamed, but cannot be shamed." But if I am transported I know it will be the death of me, therefore I hope they will pardon me.'

There is no suggestion from the trial notes that this beating had not taken place, but it was pointed out that Samuel Nelme was 73 years old and following an accident a decade earlier had lost an arm. William had stolen 10 sovereigns from him so that he could buy a watch and although forgiven it is possible that this was the incident that had angered his grandfather.

Despite the evidence of insanity from medical professionals, murder by poisoning required pre-meditation and deliberate preparation which made a plea of insanity problematic. Lord Rolfe, who was later to become the Lord High Chancellor of Great Britain, passed the death sentence on William and he was initially remanded in Holloway Prison. He was granted a Royal Mercy on 23 December 1847 and the death sentence was commuted to transportation for life. William was sent to Parkhurst Prison in the Isle of Wight until he was 16 years old, the minimum age for transportation. His mother attempted to have the sentence overturned, writing to the courts on several occasions to prevent his removal overseas which she did not believe he was strong enough to endure. Her requests were not granted and William set sail on 16 July 1851 aboard the *Minden* with 301 other convicts. The ship arrived in Western Australia on 14 October. Mary Allnutt's fears were not without foundation as William died of tuberculosis 18 months later.

Following his trial and committal, William's mother Mary moved back to Hastings. In April 1851 she nursed her eldest daughter, 14-year-old Mary

Above: London Old Bethlem Hospital at Moorfields, 1750. *Old and New London,* 1897.

Below: New Bethlem Hospital at St George's Fields. Engraved print by Thomas Shepherd, 1828.

Assassination of Spencer Perceval, *Cassell's Illustrated History of England,* 1909.

Spencer Perceval. Antique
engraving, 1846.

Daniel M'Naughten. *London
Illustrated News,* 1843.

7th Earl of Shaftesbury. *Vanity Fair,* caricature by Carlo Pellegrini, 1869.

Joshua Jebb. *Illustrated London News,* 1863.

Airing Court at Broadmoor. *Illustrated London News,* 1867.

Men on the Terrace at Broadmoor. *Illustrated London News,* 1867.

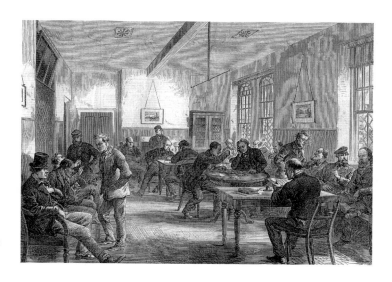

Day-room for male patients, Broadmoor. *Illustrated London News,* 1867.

Female dormitory, Broadmoor. *Illustrated London News,* 1867.

Male single room, Broadmoor. *Illustrated London News,* 1867.

The Old Cemetery, Broadmoor. *Broadmoor,* Ralph Partridge, 1953.

Sir James Crichton-Browne.
Illustrated London News,
1886.

Jane Cakebread. *Daily
Chronicle,* 1875.

Robert Coombes. *Police News,* 1895.

Above: William Allnutt in court. *Pictorial Times,* 1851.

Below: Eaton Hall, Cheshire. Frith Postcards, undated.

Above: Men's day-room, Bethlehem Hospital, 1875. *Cassell's Illustrated History of England,* 1909.

Below: Coffin Ticket, Southern Railway, London. Private collection.

SOUTHERN RAILWAY.

LONDON NECROPOLIS

COFFIN TICKET

WATERLOO to

BROOKWOOD

THIRD   CLASS

George McCondach Memorial, Fetteresso. Photograph by John Burt, 2017.

Lefroy

Above: Parkside Asylum.
Courtesy of Cheshire Archives.

Left: Percy Lefroy Mapleton.
The Graphic, 1881.

Above: Trial of Percy Mapleton. *The Graphic,* 1881.

Below: Jury at the trial of Percy Mapleton. *The Graphic,* 1881.

Lydia Gold, widowed in the Brighton Railway case. *The Graphic,* 1881.

Louisa, who sadly died shortly afterwards. Mary herself died five years later aged 42 and was buried on 1 August 1856 in Sutton Courtenay, Berkshire. Two of William's siblings – elder brother Samuel and younger sister Sarah – emigrated to Australia in the 1850s and married and remained there until their deaths. Samuel Nelme's wife Sarah died five months after him in March 1848. The couple are buried together in Hackney.

Forty years later, another two boys the same age as William Allnutt were also tried at the Old Bailey for murder. The outcome for the Coombes brothers was however very different.

Robert Allen Coombes

In 1895, 13-year-old Robert Allen Coombes, a plater's helper of Cave Road, Plaistow, London and his 11-year-old brother, Nathaniel George Coombes, were charged at West Ham Police Court with the murder of their mother, Emily. The post mortem showed that she had been stabbed in the left breast with a knife. The boys concealed her death and carried on as if nothing had happened, very much ignoring the gravity of the situation they were in. They went to Lord's Cricket Ground and informed the neighbours that their mother had gone to Liverpool to visit her family. Emily's body lay undiscovered in her bedroom for ten days.

The boys were charged with her murder, but Nathaniel was released as Robert admitted purchasing the knife and committing the stabbing.

The trial of Robert Coombes took place at the Old Bailey. Robert's father, also called Robert Coombes, who was away at sea when the murder took place, was questioned about insanity within the family. He stated that there was none in his family, but his wife had been an excitable woman and his son Robert had marks on the side of his head from a forceps delivery and regularly complained of severe headaches.

George Edward Walker, the medical officer for Holloway and Newgate prisons stated that Robert was:

> 'singing and whistling, and was very impertinent to the officers – he has complained of pains in the head on two or three occasions – he told me he had suffered from them more or less all his life – there is a distinct scar on his right temple, and on very careful examination I noticed also a very faint

scar just in front of his left ear – those scars might have been
caused by instruments used at the time of his birth – the brain
is always compressed more or less when instruments are used,
which will occasionally affect the brain.'

George Walker was of the opinion that Robert Coombes was suffering from
cerebral excitement:

'It was peculiar, he appeared in very great glee at being about
to be brought here to be tried, his manner was peculiar, but you
would hardly say he was suffering from very great excitement
that day, he thought it would be a splendid sight, and he was
looking forward to it, he said he would wear his best clothes
and have his boots well polished, then he began to talk about
his cats, from having been very talkative he suddenly became
very silent and burst into tears. I asked him why he was crying,
and he said because he wanted his cats and his mandolin. I
have his letter, which was handed to me on Sunday, which
appears to be written by an insane person.'

The letter addressed to Mr. Shaw, 583, Barking Road, Plaistow, Essex and
had been sent by Robert from HM Prison, Holloway on 14 September 1895:

'Dear Mr. Shaw, I received your letter on last Tuesday. I
think I will get hung, but I do not care as long as I get a good
breakfast before they hang me. If they do not hang me I think
I will commit suicide. That will do just as well. I will strangle
myself. I hope you are all well. I go up on Monday to the Old
Bailey to be tried. I hope you will be there I think they will
sentence me to die. If they do I will call all the witnesses liars.
'I remain, yours affectionately, R. A. Coombes.'

The bottom of the letter contained a series of drawings – 'Scene I, going
to the Scaffold, a picture of a gibbet and two figures being pushed forward
by another; over the last figure was written, 'Executioner''. 'Scene II', an
image of a gibbet with a person being hanged, and the words, 'Goodbye'
issuing from his mouth, and the writing, 'Here goes nothing!'

Robert also wrote a will which was shown to the assembled court.
It read:

'My will:

'To Dr. Walker, £3,000; to Mr. Payne, £2,000; to Mr. Shaw, £5,000; to my father, £60,000; to all the warders, £300 a piece. Signed, R. Coombes, Chairman, Solicitor.

P.S. Excuse the crooked scaffold, I was too heavy, I bent it; I leave you £5,000'.

The letter strengthened the opinion of Robert's mental condition and indicated insanity. He was diagnosed with homicidal mania.

Robert Coombes was initially sent to Holloway Prison where the medical officer noted periodic attacks of mania. He was moved by train to Broadmoor accompanied by two warders and the interested press stated that he returned the glances of his fellow passengers with a careless smile as he made the journey.

Coombes thrived in Broadmoor where he was one of the youngest patients. He joined the brass band and played cricket in the first XI. He was lucky enough to be discharged from Broadmoor in 1912 and emigrated to Australia where he enlisted in the 45th Battalion of the Australian Imperial Force in Sydney in September 1914. He served at Gallipoli and on 12 October 1916 was made Band Sergeant. His name was mentioned in British and Australian newspapers when he was awarded the Military Medal for bravery in the field on 27 October 1916. His brother Nathanial also emigrated to Australia and served in the Royal Navy during both World Wars. Robert Coombes died in New South Wales on 7 May 1949.

In Glasgow in 1888 a murder occurred which tested the Scottish judicial system and incarcerated a young boy with severe learning difficulties for life.

John Brannigan

John Brannigan was admitted to the Lunatic Department of the General Prison of Perth on 30th October 1888. John was just 13 years old and was declared to be an imbecile. He had been indicted alongside his Irish alcoholic mother, Mary Ann Campbell, of murdering his father, Thomas Brannigan, a quayside dock worker and army pensioner, aged 52, sometime between the 16 and 18 August 1888 in their house in Wallace Street, Tradeston. His father had died after sustaining multiple hammer blows to his skull. The post-mortem report recorded that he succumbed from 'head injuries inflicted by a blunt instrument' – apparently Thomas's head had 'been battered into pulp'. A bloodied hammer with hair fibres upon it was found secreted in a cupboard in the house.

William Armstrong, John's brother-in-law, married to his sister Emily Brannigan, reported that when John was a young child he had been gored by a cow and the cow's horn had penetrated into his skull – 'he had never been the same since'. John suffered physical, and very likely mental complications from this significant brain injury and he started to have convulsions. This was corroborated by medical records which noted that physically he had an abnormal skull shape with a 'peculiar conformation of cranium with exaggerated parietal eminences'. John's brain injury led to epilepsy.

On 18 August 1888, John Brannigan's sister and brother-in-law sent their seven-year-old son, William John Armstrong, with a message and a sixpence to deliver to his grandfather, telling the boy to deliver it to no-one else. However, when William John got to his grandparent's house at 52, Wallace Street, South Side, Glasgow, his grandmother shooed him away saying that his grandfather was unwell in bed. William persevered, asking to see his grandfather, but Mary Brannigan refused him entry and asked him to leave saying he could not disturb the old man.

When William returned home and told his parents what had happened, his father suspected that something was amiss. William Armstrong went round to Wallace Street but found the tenement flat locked. After obtaining a key from a neighbour and entering the apartment he discovered the appalling scene of his naked father-in-law lying in bed covered in blood with his head battered in. Thomas Brannigan had clearly been murdered. William Armstrong immediately contacted the police. Both Mary Ann Campbell and John Brannigan were arrested on suspicion of the murder.

The murder case was heard at the High Court of Glasgow on 25 October 1888 before Alexander Burns Shand, Lord Burns, Lord of Session. At the trial, Dr James Wallace Anderson of Duke Street, Glasgow gave evidence that John Brannigan was an imbecile, capable of understanding only very simple facts and very simple objects and had the mental age of a 3 or 4-year-old child. During Dr Anderson's evidence, John started to moan, groan and cry. Dr Anderson instructed that he should be laid flat in the dock because he suffered from epileptic fits. Dr Samuel Johnston Moore then gave evidence that he had examined the boy with two other doctors– Dr Sutherland and Dr Dunlop – on 6 September. He said 'the boy's mind was almost a blank – he could not remember a thing that happened two or three minutes before – he could not be responsible for his actions'. Dr Moore advised the prison surgeon, Dr Sutherland, to have a cast taken of the boy's head as it was such a peculiar shape. Dr Moore stated that John was incapable of pleading.

The Court found that John was indeed insane and could not be tried because he was incapable of instructing a defence. Lord Shand ordered him to be detained during Her Majesty's pleasure as a criminal lunatic and he was subsequently removed to the Criminal Lunatic Department at Perth.

The Court then considered the indictment against John's mother, Mary Ann Campbell or Brannigan. It was apparent that she was an alcoholic. When questioned by the police, she blamed her imbecile son for the murder stating, 'it was Johnny did it because his father had beat him with a leather belt … he struck his father with a hammer.'

However, when John was taken to the police office, he was stripped and no marks or bruises were found upon him – there was absolutely no evidence that his father had thrashed him. Furthermore, Dr James Chalmers, the police surgeon, considered John to be physically weak and gave the opinion that it was highly improbable that he could possibly have inflicted the hammer blows to his father. Forensic evidence showed that Dr Chalmers had found blood splatters on Mary Ann Brannigan's clothing.

It became apparent as the trial went on that she and her husband were not on the best of terms and had frequent disagreements. Thomas had made complaints to the police on at least three occasions that his wife had abused him. Noises of family arguments and loud quarrelling had been heard in the house by nearby neighbours.

Some evidence was placed before the court by Mary Ann's defence that, during John's temporary admission to Merryflats Asylum at Govan, between his father's death and the trial, he had over 30 fits and also displayed episodes of violence.

The verdict on the murder charge on Mary Ann Brannigan was 'Not Proven' – a Scots Law verdict indicating 'we think you are guilty, but have insufficient evidence to prove it in Court beyond reasonable doubt, but equally we do not have enough evidence to prove that you are innocent'. Mary Ann Brannigan was consequently discharged 'scot-free'.

John Brannigan spent the rest of his days in the Criminal Lunatic Department at Perth. He continued to have frequent epileptic seizures both by day and night having had 73 fits in 1895, and 70 in 1896 when he was described as suffering from 'epileptic imbecility'. John died in Perth on 14 February 1897, aged 21 years, from 'double pneumonia'. His mother predeceased him, dying on 6 February 1895 in the City Poorhouse of

Glasgow of phthisis (tuberculosis), aged 'about 60'. The death registration states that she was the daughter of Francis Campbell, police officer, and his wife Mary.

Patrick Knowles – The Stockton Boy Murderer

In 1903, Stockton-on-Tees, County Durham, was an industrial town with about 57,000 inhabitants. Situated on the north bank of the River Tees, the population had grown enormously over a 50-year period due to the iron making and engineering industries that sprang up following the discovery of local iron ore. Home to the world's first steam-hauled passenger train in 1825, the town also boasted the world's oldest passenger railway station. Londoner John O'Brien moved to the area to work as a labourer in one of the iron foundries. Despite not marrying, he and his partner, local girl Mary Knowles, lived together and began to raise a family. By 1903, they had five children, of whom Patrick aged eight years was their second son.

Stockton was a dangerous place for young children, not only due to the railway, river and engineering industry but due to an unlikely child murderer. On a very cold night in March 1903, William Cassels, an official of the North-Eastern Railway at Stockton, was walking along a path between the station platform and the Old West Stockton Ironworks when he saw two boys running away. Discovering several items of children's clothing on the ground and hearing the muffled cries of an infant, he investigated and found a child aged about two years, partially buried in a small hole near a wall covered with earth and part of a disused railway sleeper on its head. The child, wearing only a wet night-shirt, was tightly bound with a red scarf around its arms and legs. Cassels carried the infant to the station offices where it was revived and dressed before being taken to the O'Shea family in Milton Street who had been missing their child for several hours. It was a bitterly cold night and it seemed likely that the toddler would have died of exposure had it not been found when it was. The railway police made inquiries but came up with nothing and concluded that it was a 'mischievous trick by some lads'.

On 30 May 1903, the inhabitants of Stockton were horrified when a second young child was found in a similar place. On this occasion however, help came too late and the body of 15-month-old baby Frederick Hughes, son of a machinist Edward Hughes and his wife Georgina of 35 Bickersteth Street, Parkfield, was found buried under a heap of sand in disused wasteland on the site of Old West Stockton Ironworks on the outskirts of the town. On this occasion there were no witnesses to the crime and consequently no arrest was made.

A week later, on Saturday 6 June 1903, six-year-old Tommy Lynas, the son of a fish dealer from Alisson Street, Stockton was wheeling his nineteen-month-old baby sister Fanny in a soap-box on wheels outside the railway station. As they played, they were approached by Patrick Knowles and another boy, Christopher Chapman, whom Knowles called 'Chapnee'. Knowles thrust Tommy Lynas away and trundled Fanny onto Durham Road towards the Old Ironworks. Tommy ran home and managed to alert his mother, Eliza, who immediately chased after them. She caught up with the boys walking towards the banks of a stream where they had intended to throw Fanny into the river to drown her. Chapman ran away, but Eliza took Knowles to her house in Allison Street and sent for the police. Sergeant James Clews was the first to see him there and took him to Stockton Police Station.

The location where Knowles was arrested after abducting Fanny Lynas was very close to the site where the toddler Frederick Hughes had been found murdered. While in custody, Knowles confessed to having enticed away, murdered and buried Frederick Hughes. In his confession, he stated:

> 'I laid the baby down and made a hole with my hands, and put him in it on his back. He woke up when I put him in the hole and shouted "Oh mammy!" and cried. I lifted his pinny over his face and pulled the muck onto him with my hands. He was crying and kicking. He tried to get up and I put some bricks on him and a big piece of stone. The stone was slag. I then left him and went home before it was dark.

Knowles also confessed to the abduction and abandonment of the O'Shea toddler found by Railway Official William Cassels in March. After a Police Court hearing on Monday 8 June held before the Mayor, Alderman G. Thompson, and other magistrates, Knowles was remanded to Durham Gaol. Described as 'a little tattered street urchin who gained a few coppers by selling matches', he was noted to be stunted in growth for his age and in a somewhat ragged and neglected condition.

On Monday 15 June 1903, having arrived on the early morning train from Durham, Patrick Knowles stood before the Stockton magistrates – his head barely reached the dock rails. He was placed on a bench in front of the dock with a police constable on either side of him but his feet did not reach the ground. He looked pale but perfectly indifferent to the gravity of the charge against him, swinging his feet in the air. His solicitor put it to the magistrates that on account of his age he should not be recognised as capable of committing murder. The magistrates decided to leave this question to a higher court and again remanded Patrick Knowles into custody. They also questioned Christopher Chapman, aged seven. He told the court that on the Saturday Knowles had met him in Stockton High Street and told him he had buried a baby. However, Mr Agar Hooper Parkin (1865-1941) of Archer, Parkin, and Archer, solicitors, prosecuting on behalf of the Treasury, said Chapman was of weak intellect, and did not press him to answer any further questions.

On 16 June 1903, the case was heard before Jasper Barugh, Esq., JP, Committing Magistrate and Borough Justice of Stockton-upon-Tees, at which time Knowles was formally charged with the wilful murder of Frederick Hughes. He was returned to Durham Gaol committed for trial at the Assize Court at Durham on 14 July and cried bitterly as he was led away.

Knowles was examined by two doctors experienced in lunacy while in Durham Gaol and was certified insane. This diagnosis resulted in him being certified as unfit to stand trial as being 'of unsound and unformed mind in consequence of his childhood and immaturity of development, which rendered him incapable of knowing the nature and the gravity of the act of murder'. The Home Secretary of the day, Aretas Akers-Douglas intervened and ordered that Patrick Knowles should be removed to the Criminal Lunatic Asylum at Broadmoor and kept during the King's pleasure rather than face a criminal trial.

Patrick Knowles was consequently sent to Broadmoor and was subsequently transferred to St Thomas's Home Industrial School for Roman Catholic Boys at Aston-on-Ribble near Preston, Lancashire. This was one of the certified industrial schools used for the detention of convicted juvenile offenders. Patrick trained as a tailor there. When he was 17 years old he was discharged from St Thomas's 'to a person who will do everything in his power to secure for Knowles a good start in life' as he was unable to name any family or friends.

At the time of his release, Patrick Knowles' parents, John O'Brien and Mary Knowles were still living together but were unmarried. They had moved to Middlesbrough with their seven children, Patrick and his murderous tendencies apparently forgotten.

Chapter 10

Infanticide

Society has sinned against the mother, and the burning sin of shame glares upon her brow, and she seeks to wash away the stain in the blood of her helpless infant.

Benson Baker, Parochial Medical Officer,
Marylebone, London, 1865

Infanticide in the Victorian and Edwardian period was more prevalent and in some cases more accepted than it is today. With minimal support networks for new mothers caring for their babies and no social assistance, many women either from mental breakdown or sheer desperation believed their children would be better off dead.

Infanticide is defined as 'the crime of a mother killing her child within a year of birth'. Prior to the 1803 Offences Against the Person Act, child murder was a capital offence and the mother was presumed guilty and would be sentenced to death unless she could prove that the child had been stillborn. Mothers who killed their newborn children could be tried for murder until the Infanticide Act of 1922, amended by the Infanticide Act of 1938, which abolished the death penalty for a woman who killed her new born child. It applied to:

'mothers who purposely kill their own child under the age of twelve months but at the time of killing the balance of her mind was disturbed by reason of her not fully recovered from the effect of giving birth to the child or by reason of the effect of lactation consequent upon the birth of the child.'

Many mothers accused of infanticide were acquitted by showing they had previously prepared for the baby's arrival by purchasing clothing and other necessities because they expected their child to survive, thus indicating no intention to commit a crime with malice aforethought.

Under the 1803 Act, a mother who killed her child would be charged with murder but was presumed innocent until proven otherwise. The Act took into account the possibility of stillbirth or the death of the newborn by natural causes and allowed juries to return a verdict of 'concealment of birth', which carried a maximum penalty of two years imprisonment. Most cases of infanticide thereafter were either acquitted or found guilty of the lesser offence of concealment. Nevertheless, the women could be exposed to the full force of the law and cases were regularly described in the press.

There was such an increase in infanticide in the 1860s that news reports decrying the crime began to appear in the national papers. Dr William Burke Ryan wrote a landmark book on the subject entitled *Infanticide: its law, prevalence, prevention and history* in 1862 and went on to lead a delegation to investigate the statistics of infanticide in Victorian Britain:

> 'Turn where we may, still are we met by the evidences of a widespread crime. In the quiet of the bedroom we raise the boxlid, and the skeletons are there. In the calm evening walk we see in the distance the suspicious-looking bundle, and the mangled infant is within. By the canal side, or in the water, we find the dead child. In the solitude of the wood we are betake ourselves to the rapid rail in order to escape the pollution, we find at our journey's end that the mouldering remains of a murdered innocent have been our travelling companion; and that the odour from that unsuspected parcel too truly indicates what may be found within.'

In the nineteenth century, abortion was not only illegal but highly dangerous and for a number of unmarried mothers, particularly young servant girls, concealing their pregnancies and killing their newborn infants at or shortly after birth was sometimes regarded as a solution to the social stigma of having an illegitimate child – with all the economic and social burdens that this involved.

Some chose to keep their illegitimate infants but many others who needed assistance to look after their children regularly used 'baby farmers' who, for a fee, took children into their care. Many of these children were subsequently sold on to grateful childless couples in a time without regulations and official adoption agencies. Others were simply abandoned. Anxious mothers were generally too ashamed or afraid to inform the police of the disappearance of their children.

These included, Jessie King who was hanged in Edinburgh in 1889 and Amelia Dyer 'the Reading Baby Farmer' who was hanged at Newgate in 1896. Both women accepted children for financial gain and then killed them.

Jessie King

Jessie King lived with her partner, Michael Pearson, in Dalkeith Road, Edinburgh. In late 1887, she responded to an advertisement looking for foster parents of the illegitimate child of Elizabeth Campbell, a young woman who had died in childbirth. King and Pearson, calling themselves Mr and Mrs Stewart, accepted a generous fee from the Campbell family, and 'looked after' the baby for a few weeks until it unexpectedly disappeared. Answering another advertisement for foster parents, and using assumed names of Mr and Mrs Macpherson, King and Pearson fostered Alexander Gunn, the illegitimate son of domestic servant, Catherine Gunn, and took him to lodgings in Cannonmills, Edinburgh. Subsequently, the child suddenly vanished. They then moved to an apartment in Cheyne Street, Stockbridge, which they rented from the Banks family still living under the names of Mr and Mrs McPherson. In September 1888, Jessie King brought home a baby girl – the illegitimate daughter of Violet Tomlinson. However, the little girl did not live there long, and the landlords of the flat were suspicious that something was amiss. One month later, some children, playing close to the house discovered a package which they took to be a football. Initially they thought that they were playing with a ball wrapped in oilskin but after kicking it about for a while they soon discovered that the parcel contained the dead body of a baby. Forensic examination revealed that the baby had been strangled.

Jessie King was sent to the gallows and was hanged on 11 March 1889 within the precinct of Calton Gaol, Edinburgh. She was the last woman to be hanged in Edinburgh.

Amelia Dyer

The most notorious English baby farmer was Amelia Dyer (1837-96) who was hanged at Newgate Prison, London in 1896. It is estimated that she killed about 400 babies over a 20-year period.

Amelia Dyer had a history of mental illness. She had been admitted to Gloucester County Asylum in 1891 after trying to commit suicide by cutting her throat and in 1893 she was sent to Wells Asylum after showing extreme violence towards Dr Frederick Thomas Bishop Logan, who certified her as insane. Following her discharge, she attempted to drown herself, claimed to hear voices and suffered from delusions that her daughter, Mary Ann Palmer, was going to kill her. In 1894, she was once again sent to Gloucester County Asylum, being discharged in January 1895. During her calm moments she was very kind and affectionate.

Amelia was tried for child murder at the Old Bailey on 18 May 1896, and despite a plea of insanity, it was judged that 'depression in a sane person, charged with murder, is not unnatural'. Amelia was asked if she knew the nature of the crime she was accused of and confirmed that she did. When asked to explain it she stated, 'I know nothing about it; I know I am accused of this, but if I did this, I must have been mad when I did them, because I am so fond of children.'

Amelia was found guilty, a condition of insanity was unproven and she was sentenced to death. She was hanged by executioner James Billington at Newgate Prison on 10 June 1896. Asked on the scaffold if she had anything to say, she replied, 'I have nothing to say.' The trapdoor opened at precisely 9am and the Reading Baby Farmer, as she had been termed in the press, fell to her death.

While it was generally believed that most cases of infanticide were perpetrated as a result of negative moral attitudes towards illegitimacy, there were also many cases that arose due to mental health disorders suffered by mothers following confinement. Medically defined as 'puerperal insanity', this condition could lead to melancholia or mania. Melancholia, which today would be recognised as a form of post-natal depression, could lead to apathy and neglect, whereas mania could cause unexpected, catastrophic, and violent mood changes with sudden, unpredictable, explosive behaviour. The maniacal form of puerperal insanity is now termed puerperal psychosis. Victorian courts were generally sympathetic to women who were suffering from this form of insanity at the time they killed their children. Testimony from doctors was much respected, and despite the condition of puerperal insanity not being fully understood, it was believed that women could be cured of their disorders by admission to an asylum.

Without doubt, some women misused the plea of insanity to escape the noose, but Victorian alienists (psychiatrists) considered hereditary factors, family circumstances, poverty and the difficulties of mothering to explain a descent into puerperal insanity. Even when faced with the most appalling of crimes in the law courts, there remained a sympathy for these women and many defence cases of insanity were upheld to allow the 'perpetrators' periods of care in an asylum.

Esther Lack

Esther Hoare was born in Southwark, Surrey in 1824. Following the death of her father, William, of typhoid fever in about 1835, she also became unwell with typhoid and was admitted to St. Mary's ward at Guy's Hospital in Southwark where she remained for 13 weeks. When she was discharged, she went to recuperate at the home of her brother John and new sister-in-law Julietta. Esther struggled to recover from her illness and her sister-in-law believed her to be 'weak-minded' and her nephews and nieces called her 'Silly Esther'. Despite this, she managed to obtain a domestic position which lasted for about 12 months before she developed a form of depression. She became an inpatient at Clapham Infirmary and remained there for seven or eight weeks before being discharged.

On Christmas Day 1842, Esther married John Lack at Saint Mark, Kennington, Surrey. John was a porter and night-watchman and the couple set up home in a three-roomed dwelling at 10, Skin Market Place, Bankside in Southwark, which was considered, even at the time, to be no more than a narrow passage inhabited by the poorest classes.

They soon began a family, and by 1849 had had three children, the eldest of whom, John Henry, died when he was ten months old. In 1850, Esther had twin daughters, Ann and Jessie, but both girls died in infancy. Eight years later, she had triplets, James, Charles and Eliza. These babies also died in infancy. Following this multiple birth, Esther began to deteriorate mentally, she became low spirited, began to experience pains in her head and her eyesight was so poor that many considered her to be blind. Despite this, her family increased in size with two further daughters – Eliza, who was blind, and Esther, born in 1860 and 1862 respectively. By 1862, Esther Lack had given birth to twelve children of whom only six had survived.

By the end of 1864, four children remained in the family home, George, Christopher, Eliza and Esther. John Lack supplemented his ten shillings a week income by knocking up people who had to rise early – a task he shared with his elder son, 17-year-old George. The couple's eldest daughter Mary Maria, married Richard Gardner on 19 October 1864 and this couple also moved into the property having their first child, Annie Sophia Mary, the following year. The Lack family home was rapidly running out of space.

Towards the end of 1864, Esther began to experience epileptic fits, on occasion having more than one a day. These varied in severity, but she usually made a choking sound, froth foamed from her mouth and she would fall to the floor. She was confused and weakened following each attack and began to suffer from increasingly severe headaches. She was also suffering from leg ulcers and one of her legs was immensely swollen. In August 1865, she received a letter requesting her admission as an inpatient to St Thomas' Hospital for treatment. Esther was worried about being separated from her youngest children, given Eliza's blindness as 'she did not want to leave the children to the mercy of strangers'. Deciding to take matters into her own hands, she determined that it would be best if they were in Heaven where they would come to no harm.

On Tuesday 22 August 1865, after the family had retired for the night, and her husband was at work as a watchman at Page's coal wharf on Bankside, Esther began her grisly task. John Lack returned home at about midnight and hearing his wife calling, he went upstairs to investigate. What he saw so horrified him that he returned downstairs wringing his hands. The couple's son, George, went upstairs and discovered his younger brother Christopher, aged nine, lying on the bed with his hands and legs wide open, saturated in blood from the soles of his feet to the crown of his head which was nearly separated from his body. His sisters, Esther and Eliza, were also both dead with their throats cut open. His mother was standing by the window in her night dress which was covered in blood. As she stood there she began to pick dried blood from her hands. Her husband's razors were in their case on the mantel-shelf in the room and the largest one was stained with blood.

Police Sergeant Garrett Monroe Pearce attended the scene and asked who had committed the crime. Esther freely admitted to the murders, at which point Sergeant Pearce told her to be cautious what she said, as it could be used against her at her trial. Esther merely replied:

> 'I know what I am doing, I did it. I awoke a little before three o'clock, I went downstairs and brought the razors from the cupboard in the kitchen; I then came upstairs. I killed Christopher first and then leant over the baby in the bed and killed Eliza, then I killed Esther, and after I killed them I kissed the baby'.

Taken into custody, she was sent to Horsemonger Lane Gaol, Southwark to await trial.

Such was the interest in the murders that many people, predominantly women, arrived at the Lack family home 'to pay their last respects to the deceased' as the bodies lay where they had been killed until the coroner's inquest two days after the murder. Without doubt, the crime provided much interest for those inclined with a morbid curiosity and several neighbours volunteered to accompany policemen who had a weak constitution into the house to prevent them having to view the bodies alone.

At the coroner's inquest at the end of August 1865, both Esther's son George and her son-in-law Richard Gardner were required to give evidence. Richard collapsed in a convulsive fit before he could take the oath and had to be removed from the court to recover before his evidence could be heard. When asked if Esther had anything to add, she stated:

> 'I wish to say I was quite destitute, and my girl nearly blind, and my husband was ill, and I thought a great deal and I thought I had better do what I did, I only thought they would be in Heaven.'

Esther was tried on 18 September 1865 at the Old Bailey before Sir William Archer Shee, who was the only Roman Catholic judge in England and Wales at that time. Esther was in a poor state of health, and although only 41-years-old, looked twenty years older; the judge permitted her to sit throughout the trial. The jury were satisfied with the evidence they heard and declared a verdict of not guilty on the grounds of insanity. Esther was ordered to be detained until Her Majesty's pleasure be known. She was sent to Fisherton House Asylum in Wiltshire and died there two years later.

Following his wife's death, John Lack re-married on 24 December 1871 at St Jude's, Whitechapel, London. His second wife, Mary Ann Eliza Goodson was a widow and according to the parish register was 16 years younger than her new husband. This was slightly bending the truth – John had taken five years off his age at the altar. The couple had two sons, Frederick John in 1872 and Charles in 1877. John Lack died in 1904.

Although the following case is of a similar horror to the Lack murder, it proved less sensational to the press, predominantly because it did not take place in London and the family were not poverty stricken and destitute, so it was given little media attention.

Ann Wilson

Ann Wilson was the 37-year-old wife of a farmer, George Wilson. The couple had had five children following their marriage in 1853 but two had died in infancy. After the birth of her fifth child, George, in December 1860, Ann had been very unwell. Her condition further deteriorated when the new baby died when he was five months old. Ann's weakness of mind and body attracted the attention of her friends and neighbours and she was visited by Dr William Pritchard of East Retford who found her suffering from 'lowness of spirits, loss of appetite, sleeplessness and pain in the head'. He was certain Ann was of unsound mind as she was oppressed by a religious despondency and absence of mind, so she was not always aware what she was doing.

Ann's husband went to Worksop on business on 8 July, intending to return the next day. Ann had arranged to spend the day with her father and brother in the village of Wheatley, being driven there by their neighbour, William Webster. After George departed, William's mother, Martha Webster, visited Ann and saw the three children all looking happy and well, with the youngest child, Lucy sitting on her mother's knee. The following morning, William took Ann to Wheatley as arranged. Her father, John Parr, and brother, Joseph, both enquired about the whereabouts of the children and she told them that she had taken care of them. When George arrived from Worksop to take his wife home, he also asked where his children were. Ann then admitted that she had put them in the soft-water cistern at their home, saying that she had not done it on purpose and asking whether the children could be resuscitated.

Disbelievingly, he asked her how she had done it and she explained that she had carried them from their beds and they were now in Heaven. Her stunned and distraught husband listened as she described how she had drowned two-year-old Lucy first, then five-year-old William and finally, seven-year-old Elizabeth who had cried very much. Not wanting to believe what his wife was saying, George rushed to his next-door neighbour, Martha Webster, to ask if she knew where his children were. When she said she didn't, he looked in the cistern, saw his eldest child's legs and fainted.

Ann Wilson was arrested on suspicion of drowning her children. The police discovered that a mop had been used to hold the children under water until they died. Ann was committed for trial at Lincoln Assizes on 23 July 1861. The jury, directed by the judge, Sir James Shaw Willes (1814-72), returned a verdict of not guilty as at the time of the murders

Ann was acting under a command of God higher than the law. She was ordered to be detained at Her Majesty's pleasure.

Ann was admitted to Bethlehem from Lincoln Castle on 22 August 1861, where it was considered that her insanity had been caused by religion and solitude. Ann believed that if her children died young they would go to Heaven and be sure of salvation. She was transferred to Broadmoor on 30 May 1863 but was discharged considered to be sane on 13 September 1867. Ann returned to her husband, who wrote to the medical superintendent at Broadmoor thanking him for the care of his wife and reassuring him that she had arrived home safely. The couple moved to Worksop, Nottinghamshire and had another child, Mary Jane in 1869. Ann died in Worksop, in 1905.

Some women diagnosed with puerperal insanity who were considered to be a potential risk to themselves and their families were admitted to lunatic asylums in the hope that they would be cured of their condition and able to return home. For the majority, this intervention undoubtedly prevented infanticide. In a few cases however, despite having been relieved from asylum care, some women went on to kill their young children. On these occasions, asylum medical superintendents and family members who had insisted on their release were questioned in court and made to account for their decisions.

Eliza Brown

Eliza Gilchrist, or Brown, stood trial before Charles, Lord Neaves, at the Circuit Court of Glasgow on 26 December 1868. She was charged with the murder of her 6-month-old daughter, Jessie Andrew Brown on 26 May 1867 by poisoning her with laudanum.

Eliza Gilchrist was born in Kilmarnock, Ayrshire in 1847, the sixth daughter and eighth child of David Gilchrist, a grocer, and his wife Janet Andrew. When she was 17 years old, in September 1864, she married Robert Brown, a tailor from Govan at Townholm, Kilmarnock. Although the couple moved to Bridge Street, Glasgow, where Robert worked with his brother, Hugh, Eliza returned to her mother in Kilmarnock for the births of her children. Their son, Robert was born in June 1865 and then Jessie on 4 November 1866. Following Jessie's birth, Eliza returned to Glasgow but after five weeks she became psychotic suffering from insomnia, hyperactivity, paranoia and delusions. She believed her husband and their family doctor, Dr Samuel Johnstone Moore, represented the Devil, and she became quite wild with excitement.

Examined by Dr Alexander Mackintosh, Medical Superintendent of the Royal Lunatic Asylum, Gartnavel, Glasgow on 6 December 1866, she was declared insane. Mackintosh wrote that Eliza Brown was a 'raving maniac, violently dangerous, and suffering from puerperal mania'. He arranged for her immediate admission to Gartnavel as a private patient with the fees being paid by her husband. At Gartnavel, she was noted to be 'very excited, dancing, kicking, striking the attendants and singing psalms'. The attendants had to lace her in a tight jacket to contain her excitement. Eliza continued to behave violently and irrationally for a few days and destroyed a dress, a shirt and a flannel semmit (vest), and she continued to kick and strike. On several occasions it took three or four attendants to manage her.

By early January 1867, Eliza had generally calmed down and was complying with the institutional regime. She worked well in the laundry and sewing rooms. On 2 March 1867, her husband arrived at the asylum and insisted on taking her home – it was possible that he begrudged paying the fees. At that stage, Eliza was documented to be 'better but still irritable'. Dr Mackintosh cautioned Robert to take great care of her as she had not fully recovered, advising that she should be carefully watched. He was afraid that she might 'do some mischief' but allowed her release on probation – half expecting her to return at some time in the near future. He did not hear anything more about Eliza until he read the report of her daughter's murder in the *Glasgow Herald*.

From the end of April 1867, Eliza began to rise early in the mornings, sometimes as early as half-past three or four o'clock and started to sing – 'even on Sundays' which was frowned upon. Robert's brother, Hugh Brown, who was staying with them at that time, suffered severe toothache and purchased a phial of liquid laudanum from a local chemist to help ease his pain. Eliza rose early as usual next morning and poured the remains of the laudanum phial down baby Jessie's throat. When Robert got up, some hours later, he found the baby pale and lethargic. Admitting what she had done, Hugh was sent to summon a doctor. Dr James Dunlop arrived quickly and found the child unresponsive and under the effects of opiate poisoning. The doctor was unable to waken her and tried the heroic therapy of putting the wires of a galvanised battery into her hands and then passing a current. There was an initial response and Jessie began to cry. She kept awake for two hours but then began to fade again and Dr Dunlop realised there was nothing more that he could do. He sent Robert to inform the police, and to mention that he was still with the child. Jessie died shortly afterwards. Eliza admitted to Dr Dunlop that she was extremely miserable and thought she would be happy if the baby was dead and went to Heaven.

Eliza was initially held in Glasgow Prison pending her trial, but she was readmitted to Gartnavel on 12 August 1867 due to her determination to commit suicide. Her trial had originally been scheduled for 1 October 1867, but was postponed due to her mental ill-health. She gradually recovered, and a new trial date was set for 26 December 1867. The case was heard before Lord Neaves at the High Court in Glasgow, who, considering the compelling medical evidence, stopped the trial declaring that Eliza Brown was insane and should be detained at Her Majesty's pleasure. She was transferred to the Criminal Lunatic Department at Perth on 2 January 1868.

The judge made a statement saying, 'this case, like many others, has arisen out of the injudicious conduct of parties taking persons out of asylums before they were cured'. It is not clear if he was criticising Eliza's husband, Robert, for demanding her release, or the medical superintendent for allowing her discharge. In 1871, Robert Brown, described by Sir Robert Christison, Visiting Physician to the Criminal Lunatic Department, as 'a young good-for-nothing husband who first introduced her into vicious society, and then treated her with neglect' is said to have emigrated to America, dying in Buenos Aires, South America in 1871 after a short life 'of dissipation and vice'. Their son, named Robert after his father, was adopted by his uncle and aunt, Hugh and Janet Brown, who lived in Govan.

From 28 February 1873 until early 1879, Eliza was conditionally discharged on license and lived with her sister, Mrs Jeanie Morton, in Kilmarnock. Criminal lunatics released on licence were subject to several rules and regulations and were required to have a named guardian for their conditional release. Unfortunately, Eliza had a mental relapse in 1879 with restlessness and excitement and she was consequently readmitted on 8 April 1879.

Over the next seven years, Eliza's mood stabilised in Perth, and the medical superintendent, Dr John McNaughtan, agreed that she was no longer dangerous. The family petitioned for her conditional liberation, which was granted on 29 November 1886. Her nominated guardian was George Mathie, husband of another of Eliza's sisters, Janet, whom he had married in Kilmarnock in 1859. On 7 January 1887, George Mathie requested that the guardianship be transferred to Eliza's son, Robert Brown. At that time Robert was just 22 years of age. He had regular and respectable employment as a clerk in the office of John Duke, Stockbroker, Glasgow.

Dr McNaughtan, was unwilling to agree that Robert would be a suitable guardian for his mother because of his age and inexperience. However, a neighbour and life-long friend of Eliza, Mrs Mary Mair, a retired missionary, offered to be a co-guardian. This was acceptable, and a warrant was granted for Eliza's conditional release on 12 January 1888. Eliza enjoyed her freedom but brooded over the idea that if she became unwell again she would be sent back into an asylum or prison with no chance of release and would be incarcerated until she died.

In 1889, Eliza and her son connived a plan for her to flee to America where she had a number of relatives and friends. They told Mary Mair, the co-guardian, that they were going on holiday for two weeks to the Isle of Arran. Instead, they went to Greenock where Eliza boarded the SS *Hibernian* bound for Boston, Massachusetts. Robert then journeyed to Arran and stayed there for at least a week.

When Robert returned without his mother, Mrs Mair became agitated and concerned that she may have been negligent in her duties as a guardian and telegraphed the Prison Commission. Eliza Brown was immediately declared an escaped convict and a warrant was issued to apprehend, convey and deliver her to the Governor of Perth General Prison. The Procurator Fiscal of Lanarkshire considered whether charges could be brought against Robert for aiding and abetting the flight of an 'escaped' criminal lunatic, but at that time there was no offence he could be charged with.

In December 1889, Eliza was living in Philadelphia, Pennsylvania and realised that her mental health was deteriorating. She sent for Robert, who travelled to America to bring her home. When he arrived, he found his mother in a poor mental state, tired of living, but willing to return to Scotland. Robert booked passages back to Glasgow at the beginning of 1890, but Eliza became more and more restless and agitated and her mind 'gave way'. Robert had to obtain an emergency admission for Eliza at the Municipal Hospital in Philadelphia.

Robert returned to Glasgow, reluctantly leaving his mother in Pennsylvania, and on his return, he notified the authorities at Perth about his mother's whereabouts and state of health. There was some communication amongst the Commissioners of Prisons, the Foreign Office and the Superintendent of Immigration in Boston. The prison authorities purchased a ticket for Eliza's passage home. When considered well enough to make the journey, Eliza was given a berth on SS *Prussian* which departed from Boston on 19 March 1890. The captain had been requested to telegraph the Commissioners of Prisons when the ship arrived at Londonderry so that they could arrange for two attendants from Perth to meet the vessel on arrival at Glasgow and to escort Eliza back to Perth. This arrangement failed to happen and the ship docked at Yorkhill Wharf on the Clyde on 2 April 1890. Eliza was clearly of unsound mind and was certified insane and taken to Woodilee Asylum at Lenzie. When the Governor of Duke Street Prison in Glasgow heard about this, he demanded that she should immediately be handed to prison authorities. Eliza was recommitted to the Criminal Lunatic Department at Perth on 3 April 1890 and remained there for many years. When well, she was industrious, working in both the sewing room and laundry. Her mental state became stable and in 1904 it seemed appropriate to transfer her to a district asylum. After much bickering between the parish councils of Kilwinning and Kilmarnock as to which parish should pay her fees, Kilmarnock finally accepted liability. Eliza was transferred to the Ayr District Asylum where she died on 21 November 1909 from chronic brain atrophy.

Margaret Hibbert

Margaret Cellars (or Sellars) was born in Glasgow in 1843, daughter of joiner and carpenter James Cellars and his wife Ann White. By the 1850s, the family had moved to Cheshire where Margaret grew up and married John Hibbert in 1876. Her husband was a successful builder in Manchester and the couple had two sons, James Cellars Hibbert in February 1880 and John Hibbert in November the following year. The Hibberts were a wealthy middle-class family, who employed two servants and lived in a large seven-roomed house in the leafy suburb of Moss Side.

On 18 May 1884, Margaret had a third child, a daughter, Mary Elizabeth, after which she became despondent and expressed a wish to kill herself and her children. Her symptoms grew worse, she rarely slept, and on 18 July 1884, she was admitted as a private patient to Parkside Asylum in Macclesfield, Cheshire. Shortly afterwards, her baby daughter died of natural causes.

At Parkside, Margaret was diagnosed with lactational insanity and prescribed chloral and potassium bromide to help her sleep. However, she continued to suffer from delusions, ate very little and expressed a desire to kill herself because she believed she was wicked. Her behaviour became very aggressive and following an attempt to strangle another patient she was placed in a padded room for safety. The restraint continued as her condition deteriorated and she became more and more suicidal. She believed killing her children would result in her own death by judicial hanging.

Despite her fragile mental health, she repeatedly asked to go home and on 3 June 1885 Margaret's husband removed her from the asylum against the advice of the medical superintendent, Dr Thomas Steele Sheldon, who did not believe she had recovered. John Hibbert was required to sign a written guarantee that he would make proper provision for her safety and he employed a servant, Jane Young, to keep watch over his wife while he was out of the house.

Margaret did not like being watched in her own home and on 5 June 1885 she sent Jane to buy soda water while she gave her sons a bath. While Jane Young was out of the house, Margaret Hibbert took her younger son into the bathroom and held him down in the bath until he drowned and then laid him out on his bed and covered him with a blanket. She then called her elder son upstairs and repeated the procedure. Once both children were on the bed she wrote a jumbled suicide note to her father stating how she was not going to Heaven.

Returning from the shop, Jane Young placed the soda water in the cellar and went in search of the two boys. She asked Margaret where they were and was told that they had gone to their father's workshop. Unhappy with the answer as she could not find them, she sought the help of a neighbour, Mrs Peddie, who returned to the house with her. They found Margaret in the bath trying to drown herself and managed to get her out. The women again asked the whereabouts of the boys, and Margaret replied that she had drowned them, but they were not dead as they were still warm. Entering their bedroom, the women found both boys lying naked on the bed covered with a sheet. Both were dead and had a note pinned on them, 'Dear Papa, I could not stand it any longer. No blame to you. I do not think they are dead, for they would not, so We shall never meet in Heaven. I could not help it. I had a good husband'.

Margaret was taken into custody at Rusholme, and the following day was sent before the Manchester County Police Court charged with the deaths of her two children. Frederick Price, the district coroner held an inquest into the deaths at the Alexandra Hotel, Moss Side. The jury returned a verdict of wilful murder and Margaret was admitted to Strangeways Gaol to await trial.

Tried at Manchester Summer Assizes on 15 July 1885, she was deemed to be unfit to plead due to insanity. There was no doubt in the minds of the judge or jury that Margaret was not responsible for her actions and due to her mental state, she was confined in strict custody at Her Majesty's pleasure.

Following the death of his children and the incarceration of his wife, Margaret's husband remained in the Moss Side area of Manchester with Margaret's unmarried sister Elizabeth Cellars who acted as his housekeeper. He died on 27 June 1904 at the age of 55. Margaret Hibbert died on 13 February 1900.

Louisa Proud

Louisa Constance Becks was born in Aston, Warwickshire on 25 September 1861, the second child and eldest daughter of Arthur Thomas Becks and his wife Louisa Harvey. Louisa's father, Arthur, was an iron manufacturer and the family appeared to live comfortably employing domestic help. Arthur and Louisa divorced in 1874, after which Louisa and the children moved to Kensington, London and began a new life in the home of her uncle, William Thomas, a retired merchant.

On 25 March 1886, 24-year-old Louisa Constance married John Arthur Proud, a printer, at St John the Evangelist in Lambeth and their first daughter, Beryl Constance, was born the following year in Hammersmith, London. By 1892 the couple had three daughters, with Elsie Louise Amy born in 1890 and Dorothy Maud Kate early in 1892.

Following the birth of Dorothy, Louisa became melancholic and suicidal. Her family physician, Dr Joseph William Hills, became aware that she was mentally fragile when he called to vaccinate the baby on 25 July 1892 and discovered that she had tried to cut her throat. He advised her husband that it was not safe for her to remain without supervision and recommended that she should be admitted to an asylum for her own safety. In November 1892, she was admitted as a boarder to Peckham Lunatic Asylum. The medical superintendent, Dr Warner, came to the conclusion that Louisa was too insane to remain as a boarder and should be admitted as a patient as she needed to be held under restraint. He wrote to both the Lunacy Commissioners and to John Proud recommending that she be certified and admitted as a patient. Regardless of these concerns, Louisa was relieved by her husband and returned home after only a few days.

John Proud employed a live-in servant, Margaret Tally, as a mother's help to assist Louisa once she had returned home. Margaret took care of the children, and also did the housework as Louisa was unable to fulfil these domestic duties. Louisa was anxious that her children were adequately cared for, but her depression and melancholia prevented her from doing so without assistance and this exacerbated her mental health.

On 4 April 1893, Arthur Weeks of Yeldham Road, Fulham was walking past the Proud family home at 30, Avenue Road, Fulham when he was alerted to a fire at the property from the shouts of six-year-old Beryl who was standing on the pavement opposite her home. Arthur entered the house and found Louisa in the hallway with her two younger daughters –baby Dorothy was in her arms. All three children were suffering from burns and Louisa was black from the smoke and her dress burnt. Beryl was scorched on her hands and face and baby Dorothy was very badly burnt about the face, legs and arms. Her clothes were burnt and hanging in shreds and the hair singed off her head. Arthur helped Louisa and her three children into a cab and went with them to West London Hospital. He asked Louisa how the blaze had started and she replied that she had set it on fire herself 'to do away with her children, because she thought they would be better off'.

Also alerted to the fire was Police Constable James Smith, who was patrolling nearby. He entered the property and running upstairs found there were two rooms on fire, with flames coming from under the bed in the front room. He called the fire brigade who discovered that a baby's bassinette was on fire at the side of the bed. Putting out the fire, PC Smith was able to re-enter the property. There he found a quantity of burnt newspapers, pieces of burnt cloth and a bottle marked 'Poison'.

Doctors at the West London Hospital asked Louisa how the fire had started, and she confirmed that she had done it herself as she believed her daughters would be better off in Heaven where they would become angels. She also admitted that she had taken poison in an attempt to kill herself. She was given an emetic to empty her stomach. Baby Dorothy died from her wounds later the same night and Beryl was admitted to the hospital for three weeks having been severely burned. Elsie was the least affected, and with superficial burns was able to be discharged from hospital the following day.

Inspector Samuel Wills arrested Louisa on 6 April 1893 at the hospital and took her into custody for the murder of Dorothy and attempting to murder the others. She was also charged with attempting to commit suicide. She was detained at HM Prison Holloway before standing trial at the Old Bailey on 1 May 1893 before Sir William Grantham, indicted for the wilful murder of Dorothy Maud Kate Proud. Louisa was found guilty of the act but insane at the time and was ordered to be detained at Her Majesty's pleasure. She was transferred to Broadmoor from Holloway on 5 May 1893.

Louisa's husband, John, died in 1894. Their remaining two daughters, Beryl and Elsie, were baptised on 19 May 1895 at St Mary's Church, Hornsey. Elsie died aged eight in 1898. By 1911, Louisa, who had been released from Broadmoor, moved to 19 Wellington Square, Hastings, Sussex with her eldest daughter Beryl to live with her aged mother who died the following year. Louisa died in January 1940 in Southend.

Catherine McKay

In 1890, Catherine McLean, a 35-year-old housewife was married to James McKay, a carter. They lived in poor tenement accommodation at 1 Belville Street, Greenock, Renfrewshire, with their four children – the youngest of whom was three months old.

On 26 March 1890, Catherine drowned her son Robert, aged two, in a bucket of water in the family living room. After laying him out on the floor, she left the apartment and walked with her infant daughter, Amelia, wrapped in a shawl to Red Rocks at Inverkip Bay, seven miles away. There they entered the sea; the baby drowned but with the receding tide Catherine did not. Cold, shivering and soaked, she then walked into the local police office to report what she had done to Police Constable Blacklock. His wife gave her towels, dry clothing and warmed her by the fire. He organised a search of the shore with the aid of lanterns and Amelia's body was found on the beach.

When Robert and Amelia's brother, John, aged six, returned home, he found the tenement apartment locked so he went up to the elderly woman who lived in the apartment above. Mrs Agnes Blyth had a latch-key which he borrowed. Entering alone, John discovered his young brother Robert's body lying dead on the floor. He rushed upstairs in a state of panic to fetch Mrs Blyth. John's traumatic experiences did not end there. Two days after the murders, he was taken to Greenock Police Office with Mrs Blyth to identify the bodies of his dead baby sister and brother prior to their post-mortem examinations.

Catherine McKay seemed quite unconcerned about the death of her children. She was brought up at the Police Court on 28 March and was remitted to the Sheriff Court charged with the murders. Appearing dazed and unaware of her terrible position, she told the police that she was suspicious of her neighbours and her midwife, believing that they despised her for some imaginary immoral conduct.

Dr John Robert Black, prison surgeon at Greenock, described Catherine McKay as a 'dull middle-aged insane woman with a worn anxious expression', and believed that she was of unsound mind. She was irritable and had delusions of persecution. Dr David Yellowlees, Medical Superintendent of the Royal Asylum of Glasgow, also considered her insane, and believed that she was suffering from lactational insanity. The medical officers also noted Catherine's family history of mental illness – her mother and sister were insane, with her sister currently in an asylum.

At her trial before Lord McLaren at the High Court, six-year-old John was sworn to give evidence about the discovery of his brother's body and of having to identify the body of his sister two days later. Dr Yellowlees talked about insanity of lactation as a familiar disease in the form of melancholia – 'which is distinguished by unreasonable suspicions, by perversion of natural feelings, by great depression, and by impulsive and often violent conduct'. Dr Yellowlees suggested that Catherine was suffering from these symptoms. Dr Black agreed that she was of a nervous mind, irritable, and suffering from delusions of persecution. Lord McLean spoke to the jury and advised that it was 'competent for them to find that the prisoner was insane when she took the lives of her children'. As a result, the jury acquitted her on the ground of insanity. Lord McLaren ordered her to be detained at Her Majesty's pleasure.

In the Criminal Lunatic Department, Catherine continued to express delusions of persecution. In December 1890, it was noted that she 'is generally dull and depressed and most miserable'. She displayed episodes of excitement during which she became very noisy with 'passionate outbursts'. She gradually settled into institutionalised life and in 1892 began to work in the washing house. She became more docile except on the rare occasions when her husband visited her. On a visit in 1893, she 'scolded him and was in a great rage the whole time he was in the building'. He does not appear to have visited her again. Catherine gradually settled and displayed less frequent episodes of excitement in the following years. In October 1898, she was transferred to Greenock Parochial Asylum to be treated as an ordinary lunatic, suffering from chronic mania. She died there on 19 March 1901 aged 45, from 'phthisis pulmonalis occurring in course of delusional insanity'.

Concealment of pregnancy and birth

Due to the social stigma and economic hardship of being an unmarried mother, some working-class women resorted to hiding the fact that they were pregnant and then killed their newborn child and disposed of the body. Until 1861, this was considered murder and could carry the death penalty. However, the 1861 Offences Against the Persons Act allowed for a lesser charge of 'concealment of birth':

> 'If any Woman shall be delivered of a Child, every Person who shall, by any secret Disposition of the dead Body of the said Child, whether such Child died before, at, or after its Birth, endeavour to conceal the Birth thereof, shall be guilty of a Misdemeanour, and being convicted thereof shall be liable, at the Discretion of the Court, to be imprisoned for any Term not exceeding Two Years, with or without Hard Labour.'

Other young new mothers abandoned their babies on the streets or on the steps of churches or hospitals in the hope that someone would care for them. The first Foundling Hospital was established in London in 1739 at Hatton Garden as a place where mothers could leave babies with no questions asked. Children were baptised and given a new name and often mothers would leave a distinguishing token with their abandoned baby as an identifying mark, in the hope that they could be reunited later.

Ellen Abercrombie

Twenty-year-old Ellen Abercrombie stood trial at the Glasgow Circuit Court on 8 May 1896 before John McLaren, Lord McLaren, accused of having strangled or suffocated her illegitimate newborn son. A special defence was entered that she was insane at the time when she committed the crime. Evidence was heard that Ellen had concealed her pregnancy and that she managed to deceive her mistress to that effect. She had also tried to conceal the birth.

Ellen Abercrombie was born on 6 November 1875 at Meadowhead, Kilsyth, Stirlingshire. Her parents were Alexander Abercrombie, a respected coal miner, and his wife Ellen Allan. Kilsyth, lying about 15 miles north-east of Glasgow, was an industrial town known for its iron and coal mining and there were also extensive lime and sandstone workings. On 20 January 1883, when Ellen was six years old, her mother died from puerperal peritonitis and metritis (septic inflammation of the womb) which had been developing over two and a half days. She was only 32 years old and there is no entry of a birth or death of any child named Abercrombie in the Civil Registration records around that time inferring that the puerperal infection was secondary to either a miscarriage or a stillbirth. The term 'puerperal' usually refers to a period of time up to six weeks following childbirth.

Following the death of her mother, Ellen and her younger sister Maggie were sent to live with their paternal grandparents – Alexander Abercrombie, a labourer, and his wife, Jane Ross, in Drumtrocher Street, Kilsyth. Their father married for a second time on 27 November 1883. His new wife was a farm servant named Mary Burns who had an illegitimate son, Alexander. He adopted the surname of Abercrombie after the marriage. The couple went on to have a further eight children between 1885 and 1899.

Ellen entered domestic service when she was just thirteen. The 1891 Census shows that at 15 years of age, she was working for Thomas Curr, a farmer at Whitegate, Kilsyth. She then worked in the household of Hamilton Brown, Coal Master of Kilsyth. She left this position in mid-1895 and signed on with an employment agency in order to leave the area and gain employment in a larger town. On 5 December 1895, Ellen became domestic servant to Archibald Kirkland, a tea and spirit merchant residing at Chrisview Villa, New Cathcart, Glasgow, earning one guinea per month. His wife, Agnes suspected that Ellen might be 'in the family way' but Ellen firmly denied this. She said it was 'her shape'. Ellen was their only servant and slept in a box bed in the kitchen on the ground floor. Mr and Mrs Kirkland and their three sons: Archie, aged 12; James, aged 14; and, John, aged 17, slept upstairs. On Friday 7 February 1896, Ellen complained of back pain but when Agnes Kirkland suggested that she see a doctor, she refused. The following day she left to visit her grandmother and some friends in Kilsyth. To the Kirklands, Ellen appeared to be her normal self that morning. She made Archibald his breakfast before leaving to catch the late morning train. While she was out, Mrs Kirkland noticed blood on Ellen's bedding. In the girl's box in the cupboard under the stairs she made a gruesome discovery. The dead body of a baby boy was hidden in her belongings with his head and neck covered with a shawl and tied with a boot-lace.

Ellen returned from Kilsyth at 10 pm on Sunday night. When questioned by her employer, she admitted the birth of the child, saying initially that it was stillborn and premature. Mrs Kirkland refuted this saying that the baby appeared full-term. Ellen then admitted that the child had been born alive and she had suffocated him. She said that she intended to rise early on Monday morning and bury his body in the garden.

Archibald Kirkland reported the case to the police the following morning. Police Sergeant John Tosh of the Renfrewshire Constabulary attended and charged Ellen with murder and took her into custody. Ellen made a voluntary statement that she had given birth to a baby boy at about 2 am on Saturday morning. Afraid that he would 'squeal' and wake the household, she put her fingers down his throat and held them there until he was quiet, then 'got the scissors to cut the navel string'. She then fell asleep with the baby in her arms. Waking about 6 am, she rose and put the baby in her box. Ellen added that the afterbirth did not come away until after she left the Kirklands' house on the Saturday morning. She disposed of it in the lavatory of a restaurant in Renfrew Street, Glasgow on her way to Kilsyth.

At her trial, Archibald Kirkland said that Ellen was a good servant, quiet and respectable with a kindly nature. Dr John Carswell, lecturer on mental diseases at Anderson's College, Glasgow and Assistant Physician at Woodilee Asylum, Barony, Dunbartonshire, gave evidence that in his experience he noticed in some cases immediately after delivery hysterical and emotional excitement could set in. He said that Ellen 'probably suffered from nervous and mental shock and depression, during which she was in a condition of stupor'. Dr Landel Rose Oswald, Senior Assistant Physician at the Royal Asylum of Glasgow gave similar evidence. The judge, Lord McLaren, did not believe in her insanity and gave direction to the jury. He felt that the plea of insanity had failed and suggested to the jury that they should bring in a verdict of culpable homicide. After a trial lasting over six hours, the jury, by a majority, found Ellen Abercrombie not guilty on the ground of temporary insanity. The verdict was received with applause in the court. Lord McLaren was not pleased with this verdict as, by law, he had to acquit her and order her to be detained indefinitely during Her Majesty's pleasure. Ellen was admitted to the Criminal Lunatic Department at Perth on 12 May 1896.

The Secretary for Scotland, Alexander Bruce, 6th Lord Balfour of Burleigh, feeling sympathetic to Ellen's case, found difficulty in proposing a minimum period for her detention. He sought a report from the trial judge. Lord McLaren wrote to him on 14 May 1896:

'No attempt was made to prove that the woman had shewn signs of insanity, either before or after the act; and it is not in dispute that she suffocated the child immediately after given it birth, and had tried to conceal the fact of having given birth to the child.

'Two medical gentlemen of experience gave evidence to the effect that the woman while suffering from the pain and weakness incident to child-birth, might have been seized with an insane impulse to destroy the child; but this evidence was merely theoretical, and not supported, either by reading or by cases falling within the personal experience of the medical witnesses.

'In these circumstances I advised the Jury that in my opinion the defence of insanity had failed; but I added that it was always within the province of a jury in dealing with a charge of murder to bring in a verdict of Culpable Homicide, and if they thought that woman, though not insane was so weakened by suffering that she was not in full possession of her judgement or fully aware of what she was doing a verdict of culpable homicide would meet the justice of this case.

'The Jury, however, acquitted the woman on the ground of insanity, meaning, I have no doubt, to take the most lenient view possible of the case. The result of their verdict is that the woman is sentenced to imprisonment for an indefinite time, and cannot be liberated except under a commutation of the Sentence.

'If I may be allowed to suggest, I think that as the woman is sane and as there is really no ground for apprehending danger to herself or others, it would not be just that she should be kept in prison for a longer term than the term to which she would have been sentenced under a conviction of culpable homicide. I think a fair sentence in all the circumstances would be one of two years imprisonment and if your Lordship should agree with my general view of the case, perhaps you would make the necessary order for her liberation after a suitable period of detention in prison.'

Lord Balfour gave instructions for Ellen to be closely watched and for a report on her mental and bodily health to be furnished six months after her admission to Perth. Consequently, Dr John McNaughtan, the Medical Superintendent made a report on 14 November 1896:

'I have never detected the slightest indication of insanity. She is a bright intelligent girl. I would strongly recommend her for liberation as continued residence in a Lunatic Establishment can have anything but a good effect upon a young impressionable brain.'

John Campbell, the governor of Perth Prison appended his agreement to Dr McNaughtan's report. However, the Lord Advocate, Andrew Graham Murray, thought that it would be outrageous to liberate Ellen Abercrombie just six months after 'a crime such as hers'. He felt it would send the wrong message to society and encourage other girls to commit infanticide and claim temporary insanity as an excuse. He agreed with Lord McLaren that she should serve at least two years. There was much correspondence between the Lord Advocate's Office and that of the Secretary of Scotland proposing that she could be transferred from the Criminal Lunatic Department to the penal side of Perth Prison, changing her status from 'lunatic' to 'prisoner'. This was completely rejected by the Scottish Office as it would be seen as a reversal of the verdict of the jury – totally unconstitutional and would possibly be viewed as political interference to the legal system.

The solicitor acting for Ellen Abercrombie, William Walker wrote to the Secretary for Scotland asking him the outcome of the six month review. The Lord Advocate clearly wanted to cover up the medical report from Dr McNaughtan that said that continued confinement would be detrimental to her health and wellbeing. The Under-Secretary for Scotland replied to Walker on 30 January 1897:

> 'His Lordship has carefully considered the whole circumstances of the case and does not feel able to recommend that she be released at present.
>
> 'I am further to state that the Secretary for Scotland cannot inform you of the terms of the medical report which he has received in regard to the prisoner's health, as such reports are only obtained for his confidential information and consideration.'

It was reported in the press in February 1897 that her MP, James Caldwell, was bringing pressure to bear on the Lord Advocate for her liberation. The Provost and the Church of Scotland minister of Kilsyth also petitioned him for Ellen's release.

The Secretary for Scotland sought a further report in May 1897. Dr McNaughtan again recommended her conditional liberation and this was supported by a report from the governor of Perth Prison. Conditional discharge meant that Ellen would be sent to live in the household of a legal guardian. The guardian would have to send monthly reports to the Lunacy Commission concerning her physical and mental health, her behaviour, and to report if there were any signs of insanity. Also, she would be visited four times a year by the medical superintendent of the asylum and reports would be sent to the Lunacy Commission. John McNaughtan found a potential guardian for Ellen – his brother-in-law. On 4 June 1897, she was conditionally liberated into the care of George Pilkington, Corry Lea Farm, by Bankfoot, Perthshire, husband of Mary Ann McNaughtan.

Ellen worked as a domestic servant for George Pilkington and fell in love with a ploughman on the farm, John Stewart. In 1899, Stewart wrote to Dr McNaughtan asking permission to marry Ellen and stating that he would be happy to take on her guardianship. McNaughtan forwarded this letter to the Secretary for Scotland giving the marriage proposal his blessing. On 31 October 1899, Ellen was unconditionally liberated by order of the Secretary for Scotland. It was noted 'she has been under strict supervision for upwards of three years and has never shown the slightest indication of insanity'.

Ellen married Stewart, on 29 November 1899. The couple appeared on the 1901 census at Easterton, Arngask, Perthshire without any children. Ellen died from phthisis pulmonalis (tuberculosis specifically of the lung) on 15 June 1906 at her father's house in Kilsyth.

Evelyn MacKay

Another case of concealed pregnancy and delivery was that of Evelyn MacKay, a second kitchen maid in the employment of the 2nd Duke and Duchess of Westminster at their country seat of Eaton Hall, Cheshire. On Saturday 26 April 1902, the 21-year-old Scottish servant stood before the county magistrates at Chester Castle charged with concealment of birth.

Evelyn MacKay was born on 27 March 1881 at New Deer, Aberdeenshire, the illegitimate daughter of domestic servant Elizabeth MacKay. She had been employed by the Duke and Duchess since August 1901, having previously been in the service of Henry Cecil Lowther, 5th Earl of Lonsdale.

On 5 April 1902, the housekeeper at Eaton Hall, Mrs Margaret Hay, found that Evelyn was unwell and sent for Dr James George Taylor of Chester. When he arrived, Evelyn told him that there was nothing the matter with her.

INFANTICIDE

On Sunday 6 April, Mrs Hay and a nurse went into Evelyn's room and found her poking the fire. Mrs Hay recovered a mass of 'charred substance' which she believed to be the burnt remains of a baby. She questioned Evelyn as to why she had kept her pregnancy secret and Evelyn replied that she had hoped to get home to Scotland before giving birth. She blamed a postillion in her previous employment for her pregnancy and claimed that the child had been stillborn. Dr Taylor gave evidence that the charred mass was indeed part of a child. At the magistrate's court Evelyn entered a plea of not guilty. The presiding magistrate was Horace Dormer Trelawny, Esq. of Shotwick Park. Her agent asked that Evelyn might be dealt with under the 1887 Probation of First Offenders Act. The bench regretted that they had no alternative but to refer her case to the assizes but allowed bail.

Evelyn MacKay appeared before Mr Justice (Sir Arthur Richard) Jelf at Chester Assizes on 28 July 1902. The indictment was 'unlawfully being then delivered of a certain child, by a secret disposition of the dead body of the said child, did endeavour to conceal the birth thereof, at Eaton, on 6th April, 1902'. She pleaded guilty and was prosecuted by Mr Walter Baldwyn Yates, who said that after delivery of the child she put its body on the fire and covered it with coal. Mr Trevor Fitzroy Lloyd, barrister for the defence, said that the birth was premature, the child was not born alive, and that Evelyn had expected to reach her home in Scotland before she was confined. Through the kindness of Miss Wright of the Rescue Home for Girls, Chester, Evelyn had been admitted to their London Home. Trevor Lloyd asked the judge not to imprison her so that she could return to the home where she was being well looked after. Miss Wright gave evidence that she seemed a well-disposed girl and was sorry for what she had done.

The judge said the case was:

> 'a very painful one to hear, but in her case she did nothing to kill, because the child was probably not born alive. However her great shame, the prisoner must have known it was wrong to put the body of a newly born child in the fire and destroy it so that nothing could be seen of it. It was made an offence against the law to conceal the birth of a child by the disposal of its dead body, because it would be very easy to do away with proof if there had been any maltreatment. Therefore the law was very clear about it, and he should like that there should be no doubt whatever that it was a crime. In the hope that it would be a lesson to her for life, and that she would try and lead a

good and virtuous life, I will take a merciful view of the case, chiefly because she has hitherto borne a good character, and because ladies have promised to take care of her and do what they possibly could for her.'

The Bench allowed her bail on her own recognizances in £20, and a surety from Miss Wright of £10, stating that she was to come up for judgement if called upon.

The Bastardy Clause in the Poor Law Amendment Act of 1834, which had been introduced to reduce the rate of illegitimate births in England, had a devastating impact on poor mothers and mothers of illegitimate children. It led to an immediate and significant rise in the crime of infanticide and concealment of birth. Without doubt it also had an impact on the mental health of many women already struggling to cope with the shame of a child out of wedlock. Despite this, it was nearly 100 years before changes were made to legislation when the Infanticide Act was passed in 1922 removing the death penalty for the crime.

However, infanticide cases were considered more sympathetically by the courts than murders of other family members that were termed parricides. The press and public reaction was less sympathetic to those who murdered their adult relatives.

Chapter 11

Parricide

There are murders of various grades; ... there is one from which even common murderers – burkers – bravoes – hired assassins – poisoners, would shrink dismayed: and this is – PARRICIDE!

The Parricide; or A Youth's Career of Crime
George W. M. Reynolds (1814-79), founder
of *Reynolds's Weekly Newspaper*

Parricide, or the murder of a family member, goes against the moral code of decent behaviour in which children, whatever their age, are brought up to respect and pay deference to their nurturing parents. In the nineteenth century, it was considered an unnatural crime – and remains so – which invariably attracted much press attention, as it challenged the Victorian concept of domestic harmony.

In order to understand such crimes, the press were anxious to make the murderer appear the victim of domestic unhappiness and the deceased relative an over-bearing epitome of evil. Portraying the crime in this way helped society understand and sympathise with the murderer's actions, particularly if it was committed to defend a downtrodden woman at the mercy of a tyrannical or abusive husband.

In nineteenth century Britain, divorce was both difficult and expensive and was only realistically available to the wealthy as it required an Act of Parliament to annul a marriage. The desire to escape an unhappy marriage was beyond the reach of most people and this led to a multitude of cases of desertion and in some cases to murder.

In the majority of cases, murders within families followed maltreatment, neglect or abuse either committed by the victim on their assassin or due to the threat of mistreatment to another family member. The exception to this rule were murders where there was no evidence of provocation apart from a diagnosis of insanity.

Uxoricide

In Victorian Britain, women were traditionally seen to be in need of protection from outside influences that may have affected their character or behaviour. Initially, protected by their father or brother, before the Married Women's Property Act of 1870, their financial assets were also protected from unscrupulous fortune-seeking husbands. The financial position of women before 1870 was precarious – everything she owned became the property of her husband on marriage – in effect she belonged to a man, initially her father, then her husband. Only when widowed did she have control of her own affairs.

Street entertainment in the form of Punch and Judy shows reinforced the power men had over their wives with an aggressive and increasingly violent Punch murdering and disposing of his opponents and regularly hitting his wife, Judy. Punch and Judy became icons of marital conflict which were enjoyed by large audiences. As a result, it almost became accepted that men should treat their wives with violence. Few women admitted the situation they were in due to social stigma and the fact they were able to do little about it in a court of law. They were in effect dependent on their husbands regardless of their violent behaviour.

However, as the nineteenth century moved forwards and women gained greater control of their own affairs, they began to take a more proactive role in seeking to redress the behaviour of their husbands. But, society and the legal system continued to perceive men and women differently – women were still considered the 'weaker sex' and consequently required protection whereas men needed more control.

Newspaper reports of uxoricide, defined as the murder of one's wife, were frequently accompanied by sensational headlines – describing the act as the 'blackest of crimes'. All-male juries were often quick to convict men despite the possible suggestion of insanity. However, some men were seen to have been mentally irresponsible at the time of their crimes and this section concentrates on three individuals for whom there was no doubt as to their state of mind.

George Henry Smith

In August 1854, George Henry Smith committed a murder which shocked the county of Kent and was widely reported in the national press as 'an appalling event' due in part to his 'highly respectable sphere of life'.

Smith was a well-connected married man, who was widely considered to be highly intelligent. He instructed young gentlemen in the preparation for their entrance applications to university. His wife, Mary Anne, was highly accomplished, a great beauty and was a cousin of Charles John, 1st Earl Canning, who was Postmaster General between 1853 and 1855. Canning secured the post of Postmaster for Jersey for Smith following a change in his financial circumstances. Smith remained in the post for five or six years.

In 1854, he began to suffer from depression, feeling despondent and melancholic. As a result, he was given leave of absence from his position in Jersey and on 4 March 1854 was admitted to Hayes Park Lunatic Asylum, which had become a private asylum in 1849, licensed to Dr John Conolly in partnership with his brother Dr William Conolly and was situated in Hayes, Middlesex. The large two-storey mansion was situated in extensive grounds with a well-wooded park spread over 63 acres. The accommodation and furniture within the asylum was of a superior class, only available to patients of the middle and higher ranks of society. The grounds allowed for good walks and carriages were kept for patients' use, as this was considered of therapeutic benefit. Smith remained there until 18 May 1854.

For about ten weeks after his discharge, he and his wife travelled to a number of towns in Kent to recuperate his health accompanied by an asylum attendant to supervise his condition. On 16 August 1854, they arrived at 22 Union Street, Troy Town, Rochester and took an apartment for a week in the home of Mr and Mrs William Holden. Once settled there, knowing that Rochester was a place the couple had lived in for many years and had many friends, the asylum attendant left them.

Once again, he became despondent and was overcome by a morbid dread of destitution. In order to save his wife from this potentially dreadful situation he believed it would be best if she were dead. On 22 August, he shot her as she lay sleeping in bed after which he quickly regained his senses and asked his landlady, Mrs Holden, to fetch a surgeon saying that he had 'done for his wife; she is an angel'. Mrs Holden also alerted the police and they arrived to find his wife lying undisturbed in bed with no evident signs of blood. Two pistols were recovered from under the mattress. One was noted to have been recently fired and the other was loaded and contained two bullets. Thomas Pearce Beavan, a local surgeon, found Mary Anne lying on her right side, a wound on the left side of her head had fractured her skull and was oozing blood and brain matter. She was still alive and Dr Beavan cleaned the wound but she died about an hour afterwards. That evening, he carried out a post-mortem and found two bullets lodged in the anterior lobe of her brain. The surgeon also discovered a phial of strychnine in a medicine chest which he believed Smith had purchased in order to commit suicide.

Smith was arrested and taken to Maidstone Gaol. His rambling statements and comments indicated that he was suffering from insanity and he was placed in one of the gaol's hospital wards. His trial was postponed as he was not thought to be competent to plead and he was admitted to Barming Heath Asylum in Maidstone which had opened in 1833 as the County Lunatic Asylum for Kent. He appeared to feel excessive grief at the death of his wife and his trial at Maidstone Assizes took place a year after her murder. He was acquitted as it was deemed that he was not of sound mind when he committed the offence. There was a suggestion that he was decidedly insane when he was removed from Hayes Asylum, and he was only released as there were inadequate funds to keep him there any longer. He was ordered to be detained in safe custody during Her Majesty's pleasure.

Smith was admitted to Bethlehem on 7 September 1855 where it was noted that he had rapidly recovered his state of mind and there was nothing remarkable or unnatural in his manner or behaviour. At Bethlehem he spent most of his time reading or in conversation where he displayed great intelligence and refinement of mind with initially no obvious signs of insanity apart from a depression of spirits. After about a year he began to suffer delusions which affected his conduct and suggested he may be dangerous. He petitioned the Home Secretary for release and made serious charges about the treatment he had received while at Hayes Park Asylum before the death of his wife. Although he was suffering delusions, a Lunacy Commissioner visited him at Bethlehem on 2 February 1860 to hear his testimony. He later apologised for the complaints he had made admitting his assertions were unfounded.

Notwithstanding, he was moved to Broadmoor on 27 July 1864. He was discharged on 16 August 1867 considered to be cured. However, in May 1871 he committed suicide at the Victoria Hotel in King's Cross by shooting himself in the head with a pistol. He was 72 years old.

Francisco Moretti

Francisco Moretti was born in 1844 in a small village community on the shores of Lake Como in Lombardy in northern Italy. His father, Joivanne Moretti, was a farmer and provided funds to send his bright, intelligent son, Francisco, to London to make his fortune when he was just 18 years old. Francisco had trained as a pastry chef in Italy.

He arrived in London in 1862 and became a confectioner, leasing a sweet shop at 105, Hackney Road. The business initially appeared to be successful and consequently Moretti made the decision to open up a second shop on Waterloo Road in Southwark. He fell in love and courted a local Hackney girl, Elizabeth Young, daughter of boot and shoemaker, Thomas Henry Young. They married on 11 December 1864 at the Parish Church of St Mary at Haggerston in Hackney. Francisco was recorded on the marriage entry in an Anglicised form as 'Francis' aged 21 years; Elizabeth was 20 years old, living at 11, Great Cambridge Street, Shoreditch.

The married couple lived in rooms above the shop in Hackney Road. However, in the following weeks and months Moretti's business began to fail and he lost money but did not understand why it was happening. Suffering from paranoid delusions, he believed that customers came in to rob him. He tapped the tills like a magician in the evenings hoping for money to reappear and, on one occasion, he dug up his garden with his teeth looking for money that had been buried there.

On 9 May 1865, Francisco Moretti went berserk. He and Elizabeth had argued the previous day, as they often did, both being short tempered, but what happened next was exceptional. As dawn was breaking over London, Moretti took a broken wooden ice-scoop with a three foot handle and a kitchen knife and began to batter and stab his sleeping wife about the head. In a desperate attempt to save herself, Elizabeth, naked and with blood streaming from her neck escaped from him, and running into the back bedroom, jumped through the first-floor window landing in a water tank. Despite her severe injuries, her desperation for survival gave her the strength to climb over a four-and-a-half foot high fence, where she reached the safety of a neighbour's garden. Seeing her escape, Moretti tried to commit suicide by cutting his throat.

Their neighbours' son, John Wood, ran to summon the police – the first constable he met on the street said he needed to consult with a colleague and ran away. John continued to Kingsland Road Police Station where he spoke to Police-Inspector Charles Webster who was an officer with many years' experience. He rushed to 105, Hackney Road accompanied by PC Bowles. The front door was barred but they managed to gain entry through the back door. Once inside the shop they found traces of blood leading upstairs to the bedroom. Francisco Moretti was lying on the bed wearing only a shirt and bleeding profusely from the neck 'with a fearful wound to his throat'– he appeared to be dead. The room showed signs of a dreadful struggle – there were spurts of blood on the floor and up the walls and the bed was in a state of disarray. Webster found a horn-handled razor, a large table knife and a wooden handle all covered in wet blood.

The police officers went next door and found Elizabeth, wrapped in a blanket, with her throat cut. Webster called for medical attendance and Dr George Haycock, a local surgeon was quickly on the scene, shortly followed by Dr Peter Lodwick Burchell. They examined both husband and wife. Moretti had a clear incised wound right across his throat about five inches in length and two inches in depth, cutting through his gullet and windpipe. Elizabeth had a triangular wound to the front of her throat, three inches by two, and her windpipe was severed. She also had swelling to the back of her head. The doctors ordered that they should both be taken to the London Hospital immediately as they had life-threatening injuries. Webster procured cabs to take them there. Both spent several weeks in Hospital.

On 20 June 1865, Moretti had recovered sufficiently to be taken into police custody. Inspector Webster formally charged him with attempting to murder his wife, Elizabeth, by cutting her throat with a razor or knife, and also with attempting to commit suicide by cutting his own throat. He replied, 'How could I when I lost my senses?'.

Francisco Moretti was brought before Worship Street Police Court at Shoreditch on 3 July 1865. The magistrate, Charles Edward Ellison, heard evidence from police, medical attendants and Moretti's neighbours who had witnessed events. He referred the case to the Old Bailey, and Francisco was remanded to Newgate Prison.

The trial took place on Monday, 10 July 1865 before Robert Malcolm Kerr, a judge of the Sheriff's Court of London and a Commissioner of the Central Criminal Court. The prosecution was conducted by Harry Bodkin Poland and Robert Orridge, while Montagu Williams led the defence. Francis Moretti was indicted for 'feloniously wounding Elizabeth Moretti with intent to murder her; *second count* with intent to do grievously [sic] bodily harm'.

Elizabeth gave evidence in a whisper, being unable to speak properly due to the injuries to her throat. She said Francisco had 'been subject to sudden fits of gloom and despondency since losing money' and that he had delusions that customers came in to rob him. Mr Williams asked her if she knew that her husband's father had died a lunatic? She confirmed that she had heard so.

PARRICIDE

Dr George Welland Mackenzie, resident house surgeon at the London Hospital, gave medical evidence. He confirmed that when Elizabeth was admitted on 9 May 1865 her life was in grave danger with her throat cut and trachea severed. She remained in hospital for five weeks. In his opinion, Elizabeth would never recover from her injuries and would in all probability require a tracheostomy.

Judge Robert Malcolm Kerr was renowned for his inclination to decide cases when only part-heard and he did not believe in juries. He declared that Francisco Moretti was not guilty on the ground of insanity and ordered him to be detained until Her Majesty's pleasure be known. He was sent to Broadmoor on 5 August 1865.

Dr Mackenzie's prognosis proved correct. Elizabeth died in April 1866 at the London Hospital, aged 21. A coroner's inquest was held to determine the cause of death and whether a charge of murder could be brought. Much of the evidence given in the original trial was gone over again. Mary Ann Smith of 11, Great Cambridge Street, Shoreditch, Elizabeth's sister, said that after leaving the London Hospital on 1 July 1865, Elizabeth had been readmitted twice. She had lived on her own means for a while but being unable to do any remunerative work in consequence of the injuries to her throat, she became dependent on Mary Ann. Elizabeth lost spirit and did not seem to care what became of her. On Good Friday 1866, Elizabeth's difficulty of breathing was so great that Mary Ann advised her to return to hospital. Elizabeth was reluctant to do so at first, but by that evening she had no choice. She died there the next day. There was no doubt that the injuries inflicted by Francisco Moretti led to her death.

However, when the coroner summed up, he said that 'it having been decided at the Central Criminal Court that Francisco Moretti was insane at the time he cut his wife's throat, he was not answerable for the result of the act, and therefore a verdict of wilful murder could not be returned against him'. The jury returned the formal verdict that 'Elizabeth Moretti died from apnoea, arising from a wound inflicted on her by her husband, Francisco Moretti, being at the time in a state of unsound mind'.

Moretti behaved well at Broadmoor and bided by the rules. He was quickly sent to Parole Block 2 as a patient who was no danger to himself or others. After a few years, Dr Meyer, the medical superintendent felt that Moretti was harmless and declaring him to be sane, contacted the Italian Consulate to discuss his repatriation.

On 8 February 1870, Moretti was escorted from Broadmoor to the consulate in London and then to Millwall Dock where he was boarded on SS *Maria da Novaro* bound to Genoa.

James Goudie

James Goudie was born in Grange Cottage, Maybole, Ayrshire on 27 July 1856, the son of James Goudie, a cotton weaver, and Sarah Logan, a domestic servant. James junior trained as a blacksmith, boilermaker and ship's-fitter and was employed in the heavy ship-building industry at Govan near Glasgow on the River Clyde.

On New Year's Day 1877, in the United Presbyterian Church in Milton, Glasgow, he married Jessie Pirrie, the daughter of Robert Pirrie, an iron moulder, and his wife Janet Crawford. Together they had four children but only one of them, a daughter, Janet Crawford Goudie, who was born in Govan on 10 October 1879, survived into adulthood. From the time of his marriage Goudie took to drink. However, in May 1883 he enlisted in the British Army joining the Royal Artillery and he served abroad. However, he was dishonourably discharged in March 1886 for 'ignominy' after striking a superior officer.

In about 1887, James returned to Glasgow to live with his wife. However, after six months he left her and Jessie heard nothing at all from him for the next eight years. In September 1895, James married 28-year-old Annie Freebairn at Dean Park Parish Church, Govan; subsequently apprehended on a charge of bigamy, in December 1895 he was sent to prison for nine months – the standard sentence at that time. The sentence was later reduced to three and a half months.

Annie Freebairn later married Daniel Fisher, a contractor's carter, four months later in April 1896 and had a son from that marriage. She died in 1939 in Springburn, Glasgow from complications following a fractured hip.

When Goudie was liberated on probation from prison, his friends encouraged his 'original' wife to live with him again. Jessie was agreeable, and for about two years the relationship was stable. Thereafter, he began to drink again and at some point, he assaulted her.

At the beginning of 1902, Goudie threatened to kill Jessie with a table knife. Towards the end of the year, when drunk, he refused to allow his wife to enter the house and Jessie was forced to move in with their only surviving daughter, Janet, who had married Richard Good, a pastry baker, on 29 June 1900 at Canning Street, Calton, Glasgow. Goudie sent messages requesting Jessie to meet him – which she did once – but when James enticed her to go to a deserted part of the street she ran away in a state of fear.

On 17 December 1902, James Goudie bought a revolver for thirteen shillings in the Trongate of Glasgow. The next morning, he called at his daughter's house as she was preparing breakfast. He talked to her about his relationship with her mother who was sitting at the fireside. James told his daughter that her mother and husband were 'carrying on an intrigue together'. She left the room for a few moments and once out of the room Goudie turned to his wife, who was only five feet away, and tried to shoot her– but he missed! He pulled the trigger for a second time, but the gun misfired. He then punched Jessie on the nose and kicked her thigh before running away. He was apprehended shortly afterwards in a public house in King Street saying, 'I wish I'd finished her'.

He was arrested, and placed in gaol. Described as a 'stout, middle-aged man with the appearance of a chronic tippler', he was tried in the Sheriff Court at Glasgow on 3 February 1903 before Sheriff Robert Urquhart Strachan on the indictment of 'assault and presenting and discharging a loaded revolver'. As the attack was made against his wife, he was charged with her attempted murder. Dr James Devon, medical officer for HM Prison Glasgow, gave evidence that the prisoner was not fit to answer the charge and in his opinion was insane. The sheriff ordered Goudie to be detained at His Majesty's pleasure and he was subsequently removed to the Criminal Lunatic Department at Perth.

Initially, James was noted to be emotional and distressed but he soon settled down and started to work willingly. The medical superintendent found him to be 'intelligent and coherent in conversation', leading him to the opinion that his mental symptoms were entirely due to alcohol. His wife, Jessie, died in Glasgow in January 1905 from stomach cancer with secondary tumours in her liver. On 30 March 1905, James was conditionally discharged under the guardianship of his younger brother, Frederick Counce Goudie, who lived in Ardrossan, Ayrshire. On 12 December 1905, Frederick reported to the Criminal Lunatic Department that James had absconded contrary to the conditions of his release. He was apprehended in a public house in Glasgow a few days later and was detained in Glasgow Prison for a few weeks before being returned to Perth in February 1906. James settled well back in the routine of prison life. He was quiet, industrious and really showed no signs of mental illness. He was conditionally liberated on 29 August 1908.

The Criminal Lunatic Department received a letter from the Shipping Company of Sir Robert Ropner and Co., Ltd., West Hartlepool, County Durham on 16 January 1909. It informed them that James Goudie had committed suicide by hanging himself on board the steamer *Yearby* on passage to Barcelona on 27 December 1908.

Mariticide

Mariticide – the act of a woman killing her husband – occurred less frequently than uxoricide – but was not unheard of. Women killers favoured poison as their weapon and many infamous cases were heard before the courts during the nineteenth century. The most prolific female poisoner was probably Mary Ann Cotton who is thought to have murdered as many as twenty-one people, including eleven of her thirteen children and three of her four husbands using arsenic. She was hanged at Durham County Gaol on 24 March 1873.

As with other cases exampled in this chapter, a verdict of guilty due to insanity guaranteed an appointment with an asylum medical superintendent rather than one with a hangman. One such case was Elizabeth Urquhart, who like Mary Ann Cotton, was tried and held in Durham

Elizabeth Urquhart

Elizabeth Dixon was born in Stockton-on-Tees, Durham in April 1841. In 1863, she married Canadian born William Charles Urquhart, who was an engine fitter from Nova Scotia. After their marriage in Stockton, the couple had two children – James, born in 1865, and Walter, born in 1872.

Elizabeth became dependent on alcohol which led her into trouble with the law on a couple of occasions. She appeared before the Petty Sessions at Jarrow in February 1884 and was found guilty of drunk and disorderly behaviour and stealing glasses for which she was fined ten shillings plus costs. She appeared before them again in September 1893 charged with using obscene language in a public place. Found guilty, she was given the option of a five shillings fine or seven days imprisonment – she chose the latter and served her sentence in Durham Prison.

In June 1895, Elizabeth, her husband, and their younger son were living at 93, Tyne Street, Jarrow-on-Tyne. Over the previous two years, William had become debilitated from a spinal tumour and was unable to work, virtually confined to bed. On the morning of 6 June 1895, Walter left the house at 5.20 am to go to work at Leslie's Shipyard. When he returned 12 hours later, he found his mother sitting on the edge of the bed telling him that his father was dead and that she was going to poison herself. Walter saw the naked body of his father and told his mother that he was going to the police. She replied, 'there will be two corpses when you come back.'

Walter returned to the house with Police Sergeant Walton and Police Constable Johnston. They found Elizabeth to be 'a strong robust woman' intoxicated under the influence of drink. She gave a statement that she had given William rat poison at his own request. PS Walton took Elizabeth into custody and she was taken to Durham Prison. On admission, she was excited and rambling, and continually said that she wished to be dead and hoped to be hanged.

There is no doubt that poverty played a part in this dreadful crime. When William became incapacited with paralysis he was unable to work and his income ceased. Their elder son, James, initially supported the family giving them two shillings a week, but this stopped when he became unemployed for 18 months as jobs were scarce.

Elizabeth was tried at Durham Summer Assizes before Mr Justice Mathew on 13 July 1895 charged with the murder of her husband. She again put forward the case that she had administered the poison with his consent and intended to take a dose herself, putting an end to all their troubles. Elizabeth was found guilty of murder but insane at the time she committed the act and was ordered to be detained during Her Majesty's pleasure. The judge was sympathetic and indicated that coping with William's long-term illness and paralysis had been without doubt, a great burden on all of the family.

Elizabeth was admitted to Broadmoor on 29 July 1895 and died there three years later on 16 July 1898 from fatty degeneration of the heart and bronchopneumonia.

Patricide

Even when victims were known to be tyrannical and abusive, patricide –the murder of one's father – inspired horror and all but one case in England in the nineteenth century resulted in the execution of the perpetrator. Little mercy was shown to offenders and the law seemed to protect the 'victim' in a juxtaposed role-reversal which the offender had tried to prevent. Justifiable homicide and insanity were the only verdicts guaranteed to avoid the noose.

William Ernest Greatrex

James Frederick Greatrex, described as a 'gentleman of considerable wealth' had been a saddler's ironmonger and export merchant to the colonies for many years. Retiring to Moss Close off Guy's Cliffe Road, Leamington Spa,

Warwickshire in the 1880s, he devoted himself to charitable activities and in 1892 was recently widowed and 74 years of age.

His youngest son, William Ernest Greatrex, was 37 years of age in 1892. He and his father had been estranged for some years, and in his youth he had been considered a cause of great anxiety to his family. Deemed to be idle and negligent of his own affairs, he spent time in New Zealand as his father's business representative. However, this was not successful, and he incurred losses to the firm which ended in his father nullifying the partnership. Determining to give him a second chance, his father purchased a ranch in Missouri for him, investing between £10,000 and £12,000. This business concern was also a failure and William Greatrex returned to Britain and began to write threatening letters to his father claiming that he would shoot him and the rest of the family as he had not been treated fairly.

Blinded by hatred and brooding over his next course of action, William decided to kill his father. Purchasing a revolver and a dozen cartridges, he travelled to Warwick where he took lodgings for a fortnight with Miss Johnson at 4, Northgate Street.

31 May 1892 was a bright, sunny, summer-like day. Old Mr Greatrex was in the habit of taking a walk each morning and as usual he left his home at Moss Close, accompanied by his sister-in-law, Miss Ryder. As he approached Rugby Road, his son, William, stepped out of a passageway and fired at him twice before giving himself up to greengrocer, Mr Bromwich, who owned a shop close by and had rushed to his father's aid. Mr Greatrex did not die immediately from his wounds and while his son was arrested by a policeman, he was taken into a nearby house and laid on a sofa while a doctor was located. When Dr Thursfield arrived, Mr Greatrex was already dead.

William Greatrex freely admitted that he had shot his father and stated, when he was secured in the local lock-up, that he had courage to shoot his father but not the courage to shoot himself. He asked for prussic acid (hydrogen cyanide) so that he may take his own life. As a result, he was watched by a constable in case he attempted suicide. While behind bars, he talked and laughed and was very composed and at ease. As he had £20 on him, he ordered his food to be supplied from outside as prison food was not to his liking.

William Greatrex was tried at Warwick Assizes in July 1892 before Sir Robert Samuel Wright. There was a great deal of public interest in the case and as soon as the court doors were opened, there was an immediate rush into the building. Having queued for more than two hours in the heat of the day, people from all walks of life quickly filled the court to witness the trial. When Greatrex arrived, accompanied by his gaolers, he saw crowds of people waiting to catch a glimpse of him. Unfortunately, the man he so desperately needed to see, his lawyer, Mr Crowther Davies, had been detained and there was a delay at the beginning of the trial. When all were present, the judge stated that the facts of the case were not in dispute but the question of the mental condition of the prisoner was one which should be carefully considered. He commented that it would be contended that Greatrex was not in a state of mind to be responsible for his actions when he committed the murder. The jury found him guilty of wilful murder but were satisfied that he was insane and he was therefore detained at Her Majesty's pleasure.

William was admitted to Broadmoor on 6 August 1892. While there, he wrote letters to his family apologising for the trouble and distress he had caused. His immediate family refused to have anything to do with him and all correspondence was conducted through solicitors. As he was due to inherit a legacy from his father's estate, solicitors were involved with his financial affairs. A request was made for maintenance by Miss Jane Violet Davies for herself and his child. This was agreed to and she was awarded £125 per annum. In January 1905, it was recommended that a life insurance policy be taken out in the event of William's death to protect the financial security of Miss Davies and their child. The insurance company sought an opinion about his life expectancy and were reassured that he was in good health and was expected to have an above average lifespan. The policy commenced in October 1905, but William Greatrex unexpectedly died on 4 December that year at the age of fifty. His cause of death was attributed to acute pulmonary tuberculosis.

John William Gavan

In 1893, Hercules Road, Lambeth was occupied by a disparate group of householders – most were poor people renting accommodation for a year or less, but others were comfortably off. The street backed onto the London and South Western Railway line and was very close to Bethlehem. The Gavan family – 54-year-old Patrick and his two sons – rented a single room on the first-floor at 30, Hercules Road where they lived and slept together. The boys' mother, Patrick's wife, Maria Claley, had been admitted to an asylum three years earlier.

The Gavan men all worked in the printing industry. Patrick Gavan, born in Ireland, worked as a printer pressman and salesman. Joseph, christened as Patrick Joseph Gavan in 1872 in London, was a printer. John William Gavan was born in London in 1875 and was employed as an apprentice compositor – arranging type for printing – and from 1891 he was apprenticed to George Young of Tooley Street, Southwark.

Shortly after midnight on Sunday 14 May 1893, 23-year-old Joseph Gavan was woken by the noise of a furious kerfuffle between his 18-year-old brother, John, and their father. By the dim illumination of the street gas-light, Joseph could see that the two men were wrestling in their nightshirts. Jumping out of bed and planning to separate them, he heard his father call out, 'I'm stabbed.' When Joseph managed to strike a light, he saw that his father had fallen on his face on the floor – and a knife was buried deep into his back. Before his brother could inflict more injury, he managed to restrain him and took him to Kennington Road Police Station at Lambeth, before running off to find a doctor to tend his father.

Dr Robert Galbraith Reid, the police surgeon, attended and found Patrick Gavan dead, lying on the floor in a pool of blood with a large chef's knife in his back. The knife was buried to the hilt just below his left shoulder blade close to the spine and required considerable force to remove it as it had a five-inch blade. John William Gavan was arrested by Inspector Martin and charged with the wilful murder of his father. On his arrest, he gave a statement saying, 'I was compelled to do it to save my life; my father and brother were conspiring together to poison me, and if I hadn't killed him he would have killed me. I intended serving my brother in the same way but he was jolly cute.'

John William Gavan appeared before the Lambeth Police Court on 15 May 1893 before Mr R.J. Biron, QC, police magistrate, and the case was continued for further examination. John was described as 'a sickly-looking youth of poor physique'. He appeared again a week later on 22 May 1893 before Mr Arthur Antwis Hopkins, magistrate at Lambeth. His employer, George Young, gave evidence saying that he noticed nothing strange in John except that 'he had a very defective memory'. Dr Robert Reid gave evidence that he did not think John Gavan 'was in his right mind' and was suffering from delusions, consequently the magistrate committed him for trial at the Old Bailey.

At the trial in May 1893, Dr Philip Francis Gilbert, Medical Officer of Holloway, Newgate and Clerkenwell Prisons gave evidence. He stated that in his examinations of Gavan, the prisoner was clearly suffering paranoid delusions that his father and brother were trying to poison him. He believed they put lice in his food, placed phosphorous mixed with paraffin in his bed and poisoned the towels he used. Dr Gilbert declared that John Gavan was insane.

During his trial it was also noted that John's mother, Maria was in an asylum. She had been admitted to Cane Hill (Third Surrey County Lunatic) Asylum on 25 August 1890 despite living within a couple of streets of Bethlehem, and she died there on 30 September 1893.

John Gavan was found guilty of murdering his father but being insane at the time he committed the crime was ordered to be detained as a criminal lunatic in Holloway Prison during Her Majesty's pleasure. On 1 June 1893, the Home Secretary, Herbert Henry Asquith (1852-1928), ordered his removal to Broadmoor.

Matricide

More than double the number of English men were tried for killing their mother than their father in nineteenth century Britain. However, a little over a third of cases were considered to be committed by insane relatives. Although an insanity verdict was not automatic and depended very much on the skill of the defence lawyer and the views of the jury, some men were hanged despite there being substantial evidence of insanity.

John William Barker

In June 1874, a shocked and curious crowd gathered at the Liberty Court House in Ripon, Yorkshire eager to witness the proceedings and examination of John William Barker, a 23-year-old labourer from Kirkby Malzeard accused of killing his mother.

John was the eldest son of agricultural labourer William Barker and his wife Ann, née Bonwell. The couple had two other sons, George and Alfred, and in the early 1870s lived in Town Street, Kirkby Malzeard next door to the Queen Head Inn, seven miles from Ripon. Up to the beginning of 1874, John had been a well-conducted, hard-working lad who was on the best terms with his family and was particularly fond of his mother. However, in February of that year he became ill and was thought to have contracted diphtheria. His mood changed, he became reluctant to work, would spend many hours of each day sitting in the house reading and his mother was becoming frightened by his aggressive behaviour. By Easter, his parents were so concerned about their son's mental health that his father went to Ripon to ask the assistant overseer whether his son could be admitted to the local asylum for a short period to help with his recuperation. Unfortunately, the man was away, and William returned home with no solution to his son's problems.

On Thursday 4 June 1874, William Barker and his two younger sons went to Ripon early in the morning. They asked John to go with them, believing that a change of air and scenery would do him good. He refused and remained at home with his mother. When they returned at quarter to five in the afternoon they were surprised to find that there was no smell of cooking nor any sign of Ann. John was sitting in an armchair and when asked where she was he stated that he had killed her by chopping her head off while she was cleaning the cellar. Disbelievingly, William sent his youngest son, 13-year-old Alfred, into the cellar to find his mother assuming that John had made up the story to shock them. William was indeed shocked when Alfred returned crying that his mother was all but decapitated.

John Barker was taken into custody by Police Constable Clarke and held in Ripon while surgeon Dr Ledgeard was called to the house to pronounce that Ann's life was extinct. Ledgeard later gave evidence that Ann's head was practically severed from her body, apparently by a hedge scythe which was still in the cellar.

John Barker was tried at Leeds Assizes charged with the wilful murder of his mother. The defence lawyer attempted to prove that John was not responsible for his actions at the time of the crime and in fact had not been mentally well since his illness in February of that year. While in custody his conduct had been closely observed by the surgeon of Leeds Gaol, who was of the opinion that John was insane. It was also proven that his maternal grandmother, Ann Bonwell, had spent time in an asylum but 'was hardly ever right'. The judge considered that after such direct medical evidence of insanity the prosecution could hardly maintain that the prisoner was sane. The prosecution assented, and the judge addressed the jury stating that there should be no misunderstanding as to what constituted insanity. If a person was so insane that they were not able to distinguish between right and wrong, then they were not responsible for their actions. This was the case of the prisoner, and the law said that under those circumstances the jury might acquit on the ground of insanity, and the prisoner would be taken care of in a lunatic asylum. The jury complied with his lordship's direction, and John William Barker was ordered to be detained during Her Majesty's pleasure. He was admitted to Broadmoor on 12 October 1874.

Following Ann Barker's death, William and his son Alfred remained within the Kirkby Malzeard community. William died there in 1881 aged 83 years.

The murder of a mother by her daughter was not common – it went against all laws of nature and was therefore unusual. If it occurred, it was widely reported in the press due to its rarity. The case of Agnes Hay in Glasgow in the 1860s also highlights the vulnerability of widowed women left to care on their own for offspring with mental health difficulties.

Agnes Hay

Agnes Hay was born in Glasgow, Lanarkshire on 28 April 1830, the daughter of Archibald Hay, a porter, and Janet Hogg. Her father died in 1853.

In May 1869, Agnes was a 38-year-old spinster living with her widowed mother and working in the sewed-muslin warehouse of Messrs James Stirrat & Co. at 129, Ingram Street, Glasgow where she had been employed for two years. Agnes and her mother lived together in a rented apartment in Kent Street, Glasgow but the lease had expired and they were required to move. On 28 May 1869 Janet took on a twelvemonth rental of a single-room first-floor tenement flat at 36, South Coburg Street in the Gorbals district of Glasgow. It was just ten minutes' walk away from the home of Agnes's younger brother, Archibald Hay, a joiner, who lived at 125, Crown Street, Hutchesontown, Glasgow with his wife, Susanna Cruickshank, and their family.

For Agnes it was an unfortunate time to move home as she was beginning to suffer from delusions and hallucinations and she started to drink in an attempt to make them go away. On the day of the removal, Agnes went to work at Stirrat's factory as usual, but she put on her bonnet and rushed for home uncharacteristically an hour early at 5 pm. Agnes's erratic behaviour aroused the suspicion of two of her workmates – Mary McKellar, aged 21, and Jessie McPherson, aged 19 – who both sensed that something was wrong. They decided to visit Agnes at her new home on their way from work to check that she was alright.

Meanwhile, Agnes, after leaving the factory felt compelled by an uncontrollable delusion to kill her 66-year-old mother. She heard voices 'from the sky' telling her to 'murder, murder', urging her onwards to be 'quick, quick, quick, and kill her'. The auditory hallucinations led her to believe that if she did not kill her mother, then her brother and his wife and their young child would be burned. If she killed her mother, they would be saved. When Agnes arrived at the new apartment in South Coburg Street she grabbed her mother by the throat, crushed it with her hands, and threw her to the floor. Although her mother cried for mercy, Agnes then repeatedly beat her head with a smoothing iron, fracturing her skull, until she was dead.

Immediately afterwards, Agnes washed the floor and cleaned the iron. As she was clearing away the evidence, her workmates, Mary McKellar and Jessie McPherson arrived at the door. Agnes told them that they could not come in and asked them to stand on the doorstep while she fetched her shawl. They then left the tenement together and Agnes, appearing to be in a bit of a flurry, asked the girls to go with her to her brother's house. They agreed and on the way, Agnes told them what she had done.

They arrived at Archibald Hay's house in Crown Street at about quarter to seven, where Agnes was noted to be in a state of great agitation. She paced back and forward wringing her hands and tearing her hair. Agnes told her brother that for two or three days she had been experiencing strange notions and had been troubled by voices crying to her from the clouds. Among these was a voice saying that Archibald and his wife and child would be burned. Believing the words of the voice to be true, she killed her mother to save her other relatives.

Archibald was in a quandary, feeling disbelief at what he was being told, but also anxious for the safety of his mother. He sent his sister-in-law, Mary-Ann Cruickshank, to fetch Dr Hugh Taylor who had previously prescribed tranquillisers for Agnes, and the doctor accompanied Mary-Ann back to Archibald's house. When Agnes told Dr Taylor that she had killed her mother, he clapped her on the shoulder and said 'poor lassie'. Archibald suggested that he, Mary-Ann and Dr Taylor should go to South Coburg Street to ascertain if there was any truth in what Agnes had said. The door was unlocked. Archibald found his mother lying on her left side on the floor, quite dead. Dr Taylor requested that the police should be sent for. After Police Constable David Fowler's arrival, the police surgeon, Dr Chalmers, was called to examine the dead woman.

Investigations revealed that Agnes had been drinking excessively for several weeks prior to the assault on her mother and that she had been suffering from paranoid delusions. She was described as a woman of slight build and low stature, with sharp features and dark hair and eyes. The medical men who examined her, Dr Alexander MacKintosh, Physician

Superintendent, and John Hay, Assistant Physician, both of the Royal Lunatic Asylum of Glasgow at Garnavel, were of the opinion that Agnes's delusional symptoms were of a dangerous character possibly due to an excess of drink.

When appearing before Sheriff Murray on 4 June 1869, it was found that her state of mind was deranged and that further legal proceedings should be postponed. A warrant was issued to transfer her to the asylum.

She was due to be tried at the High Court of Justiciary at Glasgow on 26 April 1870, but the case was moved to Edinburgh on 30 May 1870 because of an error in the original indictment. At the trial before Lord Moncrieff, the Lord Justice-Clerk, Agnes was deemed to be insane at the time of committing the crime and was ordered to be detained at Her Majesty's pleasure.

Agnes was moved to Glasgow Prison where she remained for eight years before being transferred to the Criminal Lunatic Department at Perth on 28 July 1878. There they found her a very quiet, easily managed woman and an excellent worker. Her general health began to decline throughout the 1890s. On 7 September 1897, Agnes was removed to Govan Parochial Asylum, Hawkhead, Renfrewshire under a warrant from the Secretary of Scotland. She was noted to be 'in poor physical health, frail and stupid'.

John Hunter

John Hunter was eccentric from childhood and had an 'imbecile and fatuous appearance'. His father, Robert Hunter, was a successful and well-respected stone sculptor and builder in Edinburgh. John trained with him as a teenager but was found to be careless in his work. He left his father's employment when he was 21 years old. He left home without money, tools or means and was found after a six-week search near Newcastle in a state of near nudity, dirty and in rags. John was taken back to his parents' home at 4, Lord Russell Place, Edinburgh by Samuel, one of his six older brothers.

Over the next six years, John rarely left that house, or the new one built by his father, 6, Dalrymple Crescent, Grange, Edinburgh, where they moved in 1863. John was kept virtually imprisoned. His mind was so affected that he could neither work nor attend to himself. His parents kept him indoors for his own safety and because they did not want his imbecility known to friends or the public – such was the social stigma of learning disabilities at the time.

John was fond of flattery and had delusions that he was the mightiest of men mentioned in the Scriptures. Like Samson, he believed his strength lay in his hair and refused to cut it. He frequently mentioned that he was anxious to become a pilgrim and walk from Edinburgh to Jerusalem so that his mighty deeds might be known. John appeared a simple person of a reserved and quiet disposition and no suspicion of danger was ever attached to him. In September 1865, his father sensed that John was becoming more restless and thought he may require restraint. However, Robert Hunter took no action and no doctor was ever consulted.

John clearly felt confined and wanting his freedom, decided to leave the house. On 5 October 1865, he was intercepted attempting to escape by his mother, 68-year-old Marion Hunter née Sinclair, and his 42-year-old sister, Elizabeth. Unknown to them, he was armed with an 18-inch long iron bar that he intended to use against anyone who prevented him leaving. On the pavement outside the house, his mother put her hand on his shoulder and tried to persuade him to return home. John struck her on the left side of her head with his weapon, killing her instantly. He then battered his sister, who had fallen prostrate over their mother's body. As they lay on the pavement, he struck the bodies repeatedly.

A stonemason, Joseph Brown, working nearby and hearing the commotion, seeing two bodies on the ground shouted, 'Murder! Murder!' John ran into the back garden and hid in a greenhouse. Some other masons working in the street which was being developed at that time came forward to help, but it was clear that the two ladies were dead. Joseph Brown knew the family and ran to get Robert and Samuel Hunter from their yard about a quarter of a mile away. John remained in the greenhouse until his father and brother arrived with the police. He was arrested and taken to Edinburgh Central Police Station by Constable John McMenamin but refused to answer any questions and showed no grief for his actions. Later that day, John was taken back to Dalrymple Crescent and interrogated by Andrew Jamieson, advocate and sheriff-substitute of Edinburghshire and Maurice Lothian, Procurator-Fiscal. John refused to speak and was formally committed on the charge of double murder and removed to Calton Gaol.

He was tried at the High Court of Justiciary in Edinburgh on 27 November 1865 before three judges – Lords Glencorse, Deas, and Ardmillan. John did not appear to understand the serious nature of the charges against him and sat quietly for the whole trial with a cloak drawn round himself. He occasionally looked around and scanned the faces of people in the court with 'a melancholy and half-idiotic expression on his face'. Dr James Simpson, surgeon of Edinburgh Gaol, gave evidence that he had examined John Hunter the day after the murder and found him to be a dangerous lunatic. On 10 October, John was visited by Dr Henry Duncan Littlejohn, police surgeon and lecturer in medical jurisprudence at Surgeon's Hall, Edinburgh, and Dr James Simson, surgeon to Edinburgh Prison. Both had no hesitation in certifying that John was of unsound mind. John had told Dr Littlejohn there were a great many mighty men in the Old Testament and he was superior to all of them. He believed he was under the influence of the Holy Spirit and when the Spirit was upon him he could do wonderful things. The court deemed John insane and he was ordered to be confined during Her Majesty's pleasure.

John Hunter was admitted to the Criminal Lunatic Department at Perth where he remained for the rest of his life. He died on 4 July 1878 from congestion of the lungs with bronchitis.

Fratricide

Fratricide – the murder of a sibling – was the most common of murders within this family grouping. Nonetheless, it was still considered with horror by the press and when insanity was also involved, the public were keen to witness the spectacle of a 'lunatic' standing trial for an unnatural crime. This was certainly the case when Llewellyn Edwards stood trial for the murder of his brother, Somersby, in 1862. The courtroom was so crowded with onlookers that proceedings took place in a separate room so that the evidence could be heard above the noise.

Llewellyn Edwards

Llewellyn Edwards was a gentlemanly looking young man aged 21 years who had been born in Daventry, Northamptonshire in 1841. He was the youngest son of Somersby Edwards, a solicitor in Daventry, and his wife, Isabella Easton. His mother and eldest brother, Somersby, had moved to Wales in the early 1860s and were respectable farmers at Llanon, Dwrclawydd-fach in Carmarthenshire. Llewellyn had served as a master's assistant in the Royal Navy but was wounded in 1859 in South America after which he had an attack of epilepsy. As a result he was invalided out of the Navy but continued to wear naval uniform.

On Sunday 7 September 1862, with God by his side, Llewellyn Edwards, shot his brother Somersby at Dwrclawydd-fach. When the police arrived at the farm they were shown the body of Somersby, lying on a board in the front room. He had been shot in the head and there were cuts on the upper part of his forehead. His brains were gone and the scalp cut off. Part of his brain was found on a sickle and a large amount was found scattered, with a great deal of blood and part of his scalp in the farmyard. Llewellyn was apprehended by police at Pontardulais and conveyed to the lock-up at Llanelly, Carmarthenshire.

The inquest took place at The Red Lion, Llanon near Llanelly before Mr William Bonville, the coroner for the district, and a body of jurymen. Llewellyn Edward's father was questioned and stated that the deceased was his eldest son and the accused the youngest. He confirmed that Llewellyn suffered from epilepsy and frequently talked in a strange manner continually reading or chanting psalms and complaining that he had committed grievous sins against God which he would not be forgiven for. His mother had refused to allow him to be restrained believing that she had complete control over him. His father tried to take Llewellyn to Northamptonshire to see if the change would improve his health. Unfortunately, he did not succeed in removing him from his wife and eldest son's home.

Llewellyn Edwards appeared before the magistrates at the Town Hall in Llanelly two days later. The court was so crowded that the witnesses to the tragedy had to be questioned in a separate room. Llewellyn was asked about the particulars of his crime and stated:

> 'On the 27th of July last, I was getting up at seven in the morning to join some young men, when two Angels appeared to me and asked me if I knew what day of the week it was – it was Sunday. I then remained in my bed chamber for six weeks. Yesterday I received a communication from the Lord to shoot my brother, who had broken every Commandment. I found the gun loaded in the kitchen, prepared for me. It was a double-barrelled gun. I found my brother in the yard, with a sickle in his hand. I raised the gun. He said, he was my only brother I obeyed the Lord's command. I did not tell him that I was going to shoot him. I was about six feet from him. He put his hand to his head. I fired, and he fell dead. I did not touch him with the sickle. Nobody but the Lord was present when I shot him. I have been a master's assistant in the navy. I am twenty-

one years of age, and retired from the navy about three years ago. I had been wounded in 1859, by the son of a clergyman, named Nicholas Denys, in South America. I was on board the ship Wasp, sloop-of-war. He fired a revolver pistol at me, thinking it was not loaded. The ball entered my right groin. I had an attack of epilepsy from the effects of the wound, and was invalided in consequence, and left the navy.'

The jury returned a verdict of wilful murder against Llewellyn but, following the evidence of his father, was in no doubt that he was under the influence of extraordinary delusions which had led to the crime. Shown to be in a state of insanity, on 19 September 1862, Llewellyn was removed from Carmarthen Gaol and placed in Bethlehem where his admission details describe him as maniacal, noisy and tearing his clothes. His mania lasted only a short period of time as he descended into a state of dementia and was disagreeable, dissatisfied and unsociable with the other patients and staff. After six months his manner calmed and he became quiet and orderly.

The Home Secretary made the decision that Llewellyn should not stand trial for the murder of his brother until he 'recovered his reason'. On 26 March 1864, he was one of the first male patients admitted to Broadmoor. His family continued to enquire after his health following his admission and regularly sent him parcels of food and tobacco.

Llewellyn died at Broadmoor on 16 May 1883 of epilepsy and at the request of his family was buried at Great Woking Cemetery at Brookwood, Surrey – the 'London Necropolis' – the largest cemetery in the world at that time. It had two railway stations, one for non-conformists and the other for Anglicans, and was accessed via its own special station – the London Necropolis railway station next to Waterloo in Central London.

Chapter 12

Provocation

In the *Oxford English Dictionary,* provocation is an action or speech that makes someone annoyed or angry, especially deliberately. In law, provocation is defined as action or speech held to be likely to prompt physical retaliation. Provocation can be seen as a set of events that may cause a reasonable person to lose self-control.

Robert Smith – The Fetteresso Murder, 1893:
The Urie Tragedy.

Robert Smith was born in April 1861 at Laurencekirk, Kincardineshire, in north-east Scotland, the illegitimate son of Robert Smith, a ploughman, and Mary Clark. Robert's father emigrated to South Africa soon afterwards and Robert was brought up by his maternal grandmother, Ann Clark, and her son, David.

On 14 October 1884, Robert married Janet (Jessie) Knowles Bain in the United Free Church in Stonehaven, 15 miles further north. Robert and Jessie had three sons – James Alexander (born in March 1885), Robert George (born in October 1887), and David William (born in September 1890).

Robert was hired as a cattleman on the 95-acre farm of New Mains of Urie in the parish of Fetteresso near Stonehaven in 1890. The family lived in a cottar's house close to the farm and their baby daughter, Agnes Jane, was born there in September 1892. Smith's workmates came from nearby communities – 23-year-old farm foreman George McCondach, 16-year-old William Robertson and another farm servant called Thomas Mitchell. They lived in an adjacent row of cottages colloquially named 'the farm servants' bothies'. These three men and other agricultural labourers who had worked on the farm previously took great delight in jesting, annoying and mocking Robert Smith. He initially tolerated the situation but after a while it became too much and made him very angry.

PROVOCATION

Robert Smith, who possibly had some learning difficulties, was continually jeered, 'booed' at and tormented by these three young farm workers who enjoyed teasing him and 'having a laugh' at his expense. They decried him with names such as 'bullhead' and 'cow-killer'. In addition to the name calling, the young farm labourers blocked Smith's chimney so that his house filled with smoke and they smothered the handles of his wheelbarrow with cow-dung. They also accused his wife of stealing firewood. Following a week of broken sleep when Smith had spent several nights tending to a sick cow, and after suffering further abusive name-calling, Robert Smith finally snapped.

In the early morning of 16 May 1893, enraged and totally furious that he had been repeatedly mocked, Smith took his shotgun and also went to the byre to get another shotgun which had been given to him by his employer to keep down vermin. In his agitated state of mind, he fully intended to take revenge on all three of his provocateurs. When he arrived at the farm servants' bothy, Smith first encountered George McCondach and shot him point-blank twice in the face delivering fatal wounds and killing him instantly. Smith next turned his attention on 'the loon' – a local dialect term for a 'young man' – William Robertson, who on seeing Smith arrive armed with two shotguns tried to run away. Smith seized his second shotgun and fired both barrels after the retreating lad wounding him in the back, head and arms. His injuries were so serious that the authorities thought he would die. The stable-hand Thomas Mitchell ran away as fast as he could and escaped unscathed.

When Stonehaven Constabulary arrived, Smith, who had been hiding in Cowie Churchyard, gave himself up and was initially imprisoned in the local gaol at Stonehaven and then removed to Craiginches Gaol in Aberdeen. It was thought that William Robertson would die from his injuries and so the legal authorities took a precognition statement from him which could be used in evidence against Smith. However, Robertson actually survived.

Smith was tried before Lord McLaren and a jury at the High Court in Aberdeen on 1 July 1893. There was so much public interest in the case and such a rush for places within the courthouse that the police and a detachment of Gordon Highlanders had to be placed on guard at the entrance. The judge's arrival was heralded by trumpeters. Smith's counsel, William Brown, advocate, tendered a special plea of insanity. There was some debate within the medical profession at the trial as to whether Smith was really insane. Dr John Herbert Anderson, the Stonehaven general practitioner who was first on the scene and had tended Robertson's injuries thought Smith was sane. Dr William Reid, medical superintendent of the Aberdeen Royal Lunatic Asylum for 16 years, agreed and in his expert opinion 'with much experience in lunacy' stated that Smith was not disordered in mind. Dr Reid gave evidence that Smith's actions were deliberate, and he was therefore responsible for them. However, Dr Matthew Hay, Medical Officer of Health for the City of Aberdeen and professor of medical jurisprudence (forensic medicine) at Aberdeen University, countered that Smith's mental balance was unstable. He stated that his extreme reaction to the provocations proved that he was acting under insane delusions. Dr Angus Fraser of Union Street, Aberdeen, also believed that Smith was of unsound mind when he committed the offences.

Had Smith been convicted of murder, he would have been hanged. Reflecting on the evidence, the jury allowed Smith the benefit of the doubt and unanimously agreed to a verdict of culpable homicide. He was sentenced to penal servitude for life.

Despite his plea of insanity and the judgement, Smith was initially treated as any other prisoner rather than someone with mental health issues. He was firstly incarcerated in Peterhead Prison in Aberdeenshire until 1906 where he sewed mail sacks, made mats and endured hard labour in the quarry breaking stones. By 1906, it was clear that he was suffering from episodes of acute paranoia with delusions of persecution and excited mania accompanied by outbursts of temper. The medical officer at Peterhead reported that he 'has irascible temper and episodes of ungovernable rage and when attempting to converse with him he gives a torrent of incoherent profanity and abuse'. He had episodes of 'violent excitement' which the prison authorities found hard to manage.

In 1906, he was transferred for observation to Perth Prison where there was a specialist mental health unit and in 1908, he was subsequently admitted into the Criminal Lunatic Department. Smith became increasingly demented, incoherent, and dependent. By 1922, it was deemed that he was no longer a threat and his dementia could be managed in an ordinary asylum. He was transferred to Montrose Royal Asylum where he died in January 1937, from 'senile decay and cardiovascular degeneration', aged 75 years.

Following his conviction in 1893, Robert Smith's wife, Janet Bain, disowned their three sons and handed them over to Quarrier's Village at Bridge of Weir in Renfrewshire, telling them that their father was dead. The Village had been set up by William Quarrier in the 1870s to care for orphans and destitute children. The Smith boys were subsequently sent by a steamer from Glasgow to Halifax, Nova Scotia, and then on to a Quarrier's home called Fairknowe at Brockville, Ontario, Canada, before being adopted by Canadian parents. Their daughter, Agnes Jane Smith, who was brought up by her mother, also emigrated to Canada in 1910 and settled in Winnipeg. She and her husband, Frederick Robinson, sent letters to the authorities in Scotland asking about Robert's wellbeing.

Smith's wife, Janet, formed a new liaison cohabiting with a railway porter called William Hampton. Together they had a son, William Joseph Hampton, born in Stonehaven in 1898. The illegitimate birth was registered by Janet giving her details as 'Jessie Smith, MS [maiden surname] Bain, widow of Robert Smith, Cattleman, who died 16th May 1893'. Significantly, that was the date of the murder and it is understandable that to Janet's mind it was the date Robert left her life. Janet and William relocated to New Monkland in Lanarkshire to start a new life. Their son, William Hampton, died in December 1900 when only 2 years old from tubercular meningitis.

Janet predeceased William, dying on 4 December 1924 in Stevenson, Ayrshire, and the death registration records her as 'Annie Hampton, wife of William Hampton'. The question of whether she committed bigamy is uncertain.

Joseph Calabrese

A large number of Italian-Scots can trace their ancestry back to the 1890s when many Italians emigrated from southern Italy to escape the drought, famine and poverty looking for a better life in Scotland. Amongst them was Giuseppe (Joseph) Calabrese, the son of Nicandro Calabrese and Sarah Fikini who was born in Pozzuoli, Naples, Italy in about 1865. He travelled to Scotland in the mid-1890s together with his brother, Alexandro Calabrese who was married to Maria Dominica Roselle, and his sister, Angelo Rosa Calabrese who was married to restaurateur Carlo Bernardo. The Calabrese brothers initially lived in the slum area of Hutchesontown, Glasgow, adjacent to the infamous Gorbals. In 1898 they moved out of Glasgow and set up their own ice-cream business in the small town of Kilbirnie in Ayrshire, about twenty miles south-west of Glasgow.

There, Joseph fell in love with a local lassie, Jessie McKenna (who also called herself Jessie McGregor, using her mother's maiden name) whom he had probably met in Glasgow. Joseph married her at St Bridget's Roman

Catholic Church, Kilbirnie on 28 December 1897. The couple had four children – Phelomena (known as Minnie) who was born illegitimately on 5 June 1896 in Commercial Road, Hutchesontown; Thomas, born on 19 August 1899; John, born on 27 November 1900; and Lucinda who was born on 1 March 1903. A fifth child was expected in late May 1904. Joseph was a quiet man who was very kind and well-respected in his community. However, Jessie had a liking for alcohol and became a habitual drunkard and was well known for her intemperance. She stole Joseph's money and pawned anything she could lay her hands on to buy drink and often abused Joseph when she was drunk and taunted him that he was not the father of her children.

On the evening of 13 April 1904, a neighbour and friend, Catherine Taggart, a 39-year-old millworker, went into the Calabrese ice-cream shop in Craighouse Square at 9:30 pm as the premises should have been closed but were clearly still open. She found 28-year-old Jessie lying on the floor completely inebriated with drink. Catherine lifted her to her feet and helped her to the family apartment which was above the shop. Discovering baby Lucinda lying in a cradle on the shop floor, Catherine picked her up, took her upstairs and put her to bed. She then sent Minnie, the oldest Calabrese child, to buy some biscuits, hoping that if Jessie ate them she may sober up. Catherine stayed until Minnie returned and put the three older children into one bed before returning to her own home.

That evening, Joseph, with his brother, Alexandro, and his brother-in-law, Carlo, had gone out for a drink in a public house in the nearby village of Glengarnock. They reputedly did not drink excessively, consuming only two or maybe three pints of beer each. The three men returned to Kilbirnie before midnight.

When Joseph Calabrese arrived home his wife, completely drunk, began to provoke and taunt him that he was not the real father of her children. Jessie hit him with a hatchet striking him on the chest and the children, siding with their mother pelted Joseph on the head with lumps of coal, shouted that he was not their father. After a desperate struggle, Joseph managed to wrestle the hatchet from Jessie and in a moment of furious rage he struck her with it. When his wife was dead, Joseph killed the four children by battering their heads with the blunt side of the hatchet.

The next morning, he attempted to buy rat poison from Dr James Milroy, presumably with the intention of killing himself, but his request was denied. He then presented himself at Kilbirnie Police Office where he gave himself up. He appeared to be in an excited state when he told Police Sergeant John

McKie that he had killed his wife and family. He gave the police officer his house keys. Sergeant McKie, accompanied by Constable William Cooper, went to the house in Craighouse Square. There they found the chilling scene of Jessie and her four children lying in one bed, covered in blood with smashed heads. Joseph was duly arrested and placed in custody.

He was tried at the High Court of Justiciary at Glasgow on 5 July 1904 before James Adam, Lord Adam, Henry James Moncrieff, 2nd Baron Moncrieff and a jury. Alfred Dante, a confectioner from Ayr, acted as Italian interpreter. In evidence, Dr Alexander Naismith, Surgeon to Ayr Prison, gave his opinion that 'the murders were due to an insane homicidal impulse in a man of a naturally hot-blooded passionate nature during a condition of temporary morbid excitement, induced not only by the ordinary provocation of a drunken and thieving wife, but also by the special provocation conveyed in the taunts and reproaches on his virility'. However, both Professor John Glaister, Regius Professor of Forensic Medicine at the University of Glasgow, and Dr Landel Rose Oswald, Physician Superintendent of Glasgow Royal Asylum at Gartnavel, stated that they had visited Joseph Calabrese twice and were of the opinion that he was of sound mind.

The 15-man jury found Calabrese guilty of murder but made a recommendation for mercy because of continuous extreme provocation. He was sentenced to death with his judicial hanging arranged for 26 July 1904. Three days before the scheduled execution the Secretary for Scotland, Andrew Murray 1st Viscount Dunedin, commuted the sentence to penal servitude for life. He was moved from Ayr Prison to the highly secure Peterhead Prison and was subsequently transferred to the Criminal Lunatic Department at Perth.

The Secretary for Scotland, Thomas McKinnon Wood, liberated Joseph Calabrese on licence on 4 August 1914. Calabrese reported at Sheffield on 19 November 1914, and then proceeded to London to board a ship on his repatriation to Italy.

Chapter 13

Criminal lunatics in district asylums

In England and Wales, not all criminal lunatics were admitted to Broadmoor. Many individuals guilty of less serious crimes and with shorter sentences were maintained either in gaol or transferred to a local asylum. It was recognised that sending criminals with a mental illness to a gaol did little good, but allowing them to enter an asylum provided them with the opportunity to be cared for in a way which would not exacerbate their mental health problems.

Many criminal lunatics were discharged from the asylum when their sentence had been served, but others were transferred to the pauper lunatic patient list if their symptoms were recognised as needing additional attention.

Benjamin Hancock

Benjamin Hancock was a 48-year-old widowed cab proprietor living at Childer Thornton, Cheshire. On 24 June 1887 he stole a child's horse tricycle, the property of John Meolse Nicholson of Little Sutton, Cheshire. Three days earlier he had stolen a geranium plant and a vase from the garden of Mrs Brett in Little Sutton. Tried at Chester before Mr Justice George Denman, Dr Theodore Fennel, medical officer of Knutsford Gaol, gave evidence that Hancock was of unsound mind and was suffering from delusions. The jury found that he was unfit to stand trial due to insanity and he was ordered to be detained in strict custody during Her Majesty's pleasure.

Held in Knutsford Gaol awaiting trial, after sentencing he was admitted to Parkside Asylum in Macclesfield as a criminal patient where he was quickly diagnosed as suffering from General Paralysis of the Insane, (also called GPI), a devastating and rapidly progressive neurological disease that killed many people in the nineteenth and early twentieth centuries. Victims were mainly in early middle-age, most often in their early forties. It was caused by end-stage syphilis, yet the link between this venereal disease and GPI was not formally established until the 1920s. Mental symptoms were often dramatic with intense euphoria and included delusions, typically of grandeur in terms of wealth, strength and self-importance. Sufferers of GPI often experienced hallucinations, lacked insight, were irritable, had mood changes, memory loss, and displayed inappropriate behaviour including spending large sums of money.

There were also marked physical symptoms of the disorder which included: shooting or burning muscle pains; progressive muscle weakness; impaired speech with a weak or tremulous voice and trembling tongue; generalised shaking; visual impairment as a result of unequal pupils; poor balance; and a loss of control of the limbs. The loss of control of a sufferer's arms caused exaggerated shaking of the hands so that they could not drink from a cup without spilling its contents, and loss of control of their legs made them unsteady on their feet, usually falling forwards when attempting to walk. The progression of the illness could lead to convulsions and eventually to a complete loss of function. The prognosis of GPI was bleak and always fatal. Death could occur from gradual exhaustion, convulsions, brain haemorrhage, or by choking or the inhalation of vomit if the swallowing reflex was lost.

Benjamin Hancock had delusions that he was the owner of several beautiful villas and told the staff at Parkside that he was in possession of a large sum of money. He was very talkative, providing information that he had four children, all of whom were receiving a 'splendid education' and were being taught by his sister – who was known to be both deaf and dumb.

Although clearly disbelieved by the staff at Parkside and considered to be fanciful ramblings due to his condition, his four children were in fact being cared for by their aunt, Hannah Hancock, who was indeed both deaf and dumb.

Benjamin Hancock came from a respectable middle-class background. His father Samuel was a farmer and butcher who had enough income to employ four domestic servants in his home in Little Sutton. When he died in 1864, he was described in probate documents as a gentleman and left an annuity for his daughter, Hannah. Hannah was the eldest child of the family, born in Childer Thornton in about 1833. Benjamin was six years her junior. On 10 February 1866, Benjamin married Welsh born Eliza Davies in Edge Hill, Liverpool giving his occupation as railway policeman. His position with the railway continued as the couple moved to Betws-y-Coed, Caernarvonshire where Benjamin was employed as a booking clerk at the station. His sister Hannah and her illegitimate son James, aged eleven years, moved to live with them.

By 1879, Benjamin and Eliza had four surviving children, two sons and two daughters but shortly after the birth of their youngest child, named Benjamin after his father, Eliza died. Hannah remained with her widowed brother to help look after his children, and when he was arrested in 1887, she continued to act as their guardian, providing them with a home to keep them together.

Benjamin Hancock was not displeased with his situation at Parkside Asylum and was cheerful and delighted with everything about him. He worked well in the asylum grounds but continued to have delusions and also several severe epileptic fits. Despite being happy about his new 'accommodation', on 15 September 1887 he escaped from the asylum and made for Knutsford, Cheshire where he attempted to take lodgings. His unusual behaviour alerted his prospective landlady who contacted the police. The head asylum attendant travelled to Knutsford the following day to collect him. Benjamin continued to attempt to escape but was always cheerful and happy.

In February 1888, having been in the asylum as a criminal patient for four months, an application was made to have him transferred to the pauper lunatic list whereby his care was chargeable to the county. The Home Secretary authorised this and Benjamin was moved to the county asylum at Chester where he died on 22 January 1889.

His four children remained together until adulthood – only one of them married.

Another medical condition that was little understood in the nineteenth century was epilepsy. A diagnosis of epilepsy extends beyond the physical and biological impact on the body and brain of an individual and also affects the economic, psychological and social aspects of life. Unemployable in many areas, particularly those that involved working with machinery or as domestic servants, epileptics were economically reliant on the help of others. Grand mal or tonic-clonic seizures were frightening to observe and some sufferers displayed wild or dangerous behaviour while they were having a fit. This impact would have been all the greater during the nineteenth century when medication was limited and the prospects for individuals with uncontrolled epilepsy were bleak. The prognosis for patients with any form of epilepsy was not favourable and many became long term patients in asylums and died there. This disorder was widely regarded as incurable by nineteenth century doctors.

Mary Monaghan

Mary Monaghan was a 21-year-old prostitute sentenced to three months hard labour for drunkenness and wilful damage in 1883. Incarcerated in Knutsford Gaol, she began to have epileptic seizures.

Mary was moved to Parkside Asylum on 10 September 1883 because she displayed dangerous behaviour when having seizures. It was noted on her admission that she had previously been in the county asylum at Chester although she denied this, admitting only that she had been in prison many times due to her fondness for rum. Described on admission as a 'big lazy looking woman who was dissipated and dissolute due to intemperance' – she showed no symptoms of insanity.

Mary was quiet, industrious and respectful at Parkside and on 21 September 1883 a certificate signed by two medical officers declaring her to be sane was sent to the Secretary of State. On 9 October 1883 she was given an unconditional discharge and released from the asylum vowing to lead a more sober lifestyle.

Crime caused as a result of an excess of alcohol was a problem in the nineteenth century, and it can be argued, that it continues to remain a problem in the twenty-first century. Drunkenness was acknowledged by doctors as a disease and state run inebriate reformatories were established in an attempt to reduce the number of criminal drunkards filling up local prisons. However, there were occasions when prisoners began to display behaviour that could only be treated within an asylum environment.

Elizabeth Bimson

Elizabeth Harlow was born in Derby in 1859. She married George Bimson, a striker at an engine works in Saltney, on the Flintshire/Cheshire border near Chester in 1877. By 1881 the couple were living with their two-year-old son George Thomas at 2 Boundary Lane, Saltney and were awaiting the arrival of a second child, Mary, who would be born later the same year. A third child, Frederick, was born in 1884 but died at the age of three years.

Why Elizabeth Bimson took to drinking is unclear – it may have been the death of her youngest child in 1887 – but details of her drunken escapades appeared frequently in the press and by 1899 she had been in court 37 times on a variety of charges most of which ended with short periods of imprisonment. With no apparent fixed abode, by 1891 she was residing at Chester Union Workhouse – she became almost vagrant-like, tramping the streets from Chester along the North Wales coast creating a drunken disturbance wherever she chose to stop for alcoholic sustenance. Described as an 'incorrigible lady tramp', her most serious crime was committed in Caernarvon in 1896, when she was charged with stealing a purse containing one sovereign, seven half sovereigns and seventeen shillings and sixpence in silver the property of Richard John Jones of Llanfairfechan, Caernarvonshire. Prosecuted by Mr R.H. Pritchard of Bangor, she was found guilty – despite pleading innocence – and on 7 January 1897 was sentenced to 12 months with hard labour.

She was transferred from the gaol at Bangor to Knutsford Gaol in Cheshire and remained there until 20 November 1897. Her continual shouting and incoherent statements led to certificates of insanity and a move to Parkside Asylum in Macclesfield, Cheshire. She was restless and violent on admission and had to be carried most of the way to the ward. Diagnosed with mania as a result of drink and also with slight bronchitis, she rarely slept – despite the aid of sedatives – frequently tore her bedding and clothes but maintained a healthy appetite. She was deemed to be recovered on 6 January 1898 and released.

Elizabeth was not readmitted to an asylum, but her drunken behaviour continued as did her court appearances and spells in gaol. She died in Chester in 1918, the same year as her husband although the couple had not lived together for many years.

Severe illness occasionally caused low mental well-being and lack of appetite. If the condition was very serious and the patient struggled to speak coherently, this was sometimes confused with melancholia, symptoms of which could lead to abnormal levels of depressed mood, anguish, and disturbed sleep and appetite. Melancholia regularly required specialist treatment in an asylum.

Edward Knott

Edward Knott was a 36-year-old married labourer who had been convicted of stealing on several occasions. His first brush with the law was in January 1872 when he was convicted of poaching and spent 14 days in Knutsford Gaol. He had also been convicted several times of poaching in Manchester.

His temptation to steal again came on 19 November 1885, when he stole two ferrets, the property of Nicholas Harding of Rainow, Macclesfield. He pleaded guilty and was sentenced to four months hard labour on 6 January 1886 at Chester County Sessions.

Some forms of hard labour were considered to be useful – in Knutsford Gaol, wool-picking was favoured and described by one inmate as 'irksome an employment as any used'. However other forms of hard labour had no purpose other than teaching prisoners a lesson. The treadmill, where prisoners spent hours each day stepping up a series of steps which dropped beneath them and the crank machine, which consisted of spending large amounts of time turning a handle that produced no result. These were considered by many doctors to cause unnecessary injury to prisoners who then required medical treatment.

With less than a month of his sentence to serve, the prison authorities sent Edward Knott to Parkside Asylum in Macclesfield, Cheshire as he had become dispirited and was refusing to take any food. A medical assessment was carried out and he was confirmed to be extremely emaciated and undergoing 'severe bodily suffering'. He was in a state of almost complete collapse, had fluid in both lungs and was unable to stand. Mental weakness prevented him from answering any questions and his pulse and temperature were both elevated. His eyes were deeply sunken which gave him a fierce expression.

The staff at Parkside gave him a warm bath, fed him with beef tea, milk and a stimulant and put him to bed where he was monitored throughout the night. He tried to speak but struggled with the effort and was coughing up blood in small quantities which was believed to be as a result of the impairment to his lungs. His condition worsened and he died three days after his admission of phthisis pulmonalis. The diagnosis was confirmed as a result of a post mortem examination. An inquest into his death was ordered and it was ascertained that he had died from a disease of the lungs of several weeks standing.

Chapter 14

Insane but hanged

In February 1883, Dr Lyttleton Stewart Forbes Winslow delivered an address at the Medical Union in London on insanity in criminal cases. Dr Winslow was an eminent British psychiatrist and expert on matters of legal sanity. In 1890, he founded the British Hospital for Mental Disorders and Brain Diseases in London and was a lecturer on insanity at Charing Cross Hospital. He also wrote several respected books on insanity including *A Handbook for Attendants on the Insane* in 1877. His message was clear – 'the doctrine of right and wrong, had caused many a wretched man to meet the fate of a common criminal, though a lunatic in the common acceptance of the term'.

Dr Winslow was called on many occasions as an expert medical witness in trials where insanity was suspected, including those of Amelia Dyer (see Chapter 10), Percy Lefroy Mapleton and Charles Taylor, as well as being involved in perhaps the most notorious case of the nineteenth century, Jack the Ripper.

Percy Lefroy Mapleton

Percy Lefroy Mapleton was the youngest child and only son of Staff Commander Henry Mapleton, Royal Navy, and his wife Mary Trent Mapleton whose father, William Henry Seale, was Colonial Secretary of the island of St Helena. Henry and Mary married there on 21 September 1843.

Percy was born in Peckham Rye, London on 23 February 1860, a brother for Mary Emily Beaucamp and Eliza Julia Travers (known as Julia) who were respectively 15 and 13 years older than him. Both had been born on St Helena, as had their mother in 1825. Their mother died when Percy was only six years old and she was buried on 12 June 1866 in Nunhead Cemetery, Southwark, London. The responsibility of Percy's care was passed to his great uncle, Archibald Alexander Seale, who also died in 1866 and his wife

Sarah Maria Seale née Gladwin. Percy was therefore brought up in the same household as his second cousins Francis and Annie Seale.

Percy was not a physically strong child being described as 'pale and puny'. He suffered repeated attacks of bronchitis and was educated at home until he was seven years old. Due to his delicate health, physical exercise was not encouraged and he began to write and showed an interest in the theatre. As he matured, he developed a strong imagination and a propensity to tell lies which he always described as temptations by the Devil.

By 1878, Percy began a ruse to assist him in gaining the affections of a well-known actress with whom he had become besotted. He referred to her as 'May Gordon' but in fact it is likely that she was the celebrated actress Violet Cameron. In an attempt to get to know her, Percy tried to gain entrance to the theatrical world as a playwright. Seeking to impress, he wrote to a large number of well-known actors and actresses with offers to engage them in a comedy called 'Artful Cards'. Claiming to have secured bookings in prestigious theatres, as many as 60 actors were taken in by his deception. However, the scam was doomed to failure from the start as Percy had no play to perform and had spent a large sum of money in postage and advertising.

To avoid repercussions, his family believed it to be in his best interests to send him to Australia in the hope of obtaining employment. He was provided with letters of introduction to the Bishop of Melbourne and to a manager of a national bank and set sail at the beginning of 1879, arriving in Victoria two months later. When he arrived, he possessed only £35 which he quickly spent enjoying himself going to theatres and concerts. Becoming virtually penniless and having to sell most of his clothes, he started to sleep in parks and under boats and asked his family to secure him a passage back to England. In July 1879, barely four months after his arrival, he set sail on the *True Briton* bound for London where once again he determined to enter the world of theatre or journalism.

On 5 August 1879, and with Percy still on board ship, his father, Henry Mapleton, passed away, leaving what remained of his estate to his daughters Mary and Julia. Mary Mapleton had married John William Parker Brickwood on 19 February 1870 and by 1879 the couple had six children but Mary had petitioned for divorce on grounds of her husband's unreasonable behaviour and adultery. Julia was unmarried and the matron of a fever hospital in Islington, London. Unable to make his home with either of them, Percy once again turned to the Seale family whom he had lived with as a child. Francis Seale was unmarried, but Annie had married Thomas Graham Clayton on 16 August 1873 and ran a school at 4, Cathcart Road, Wallington, Croydon. Percy moved in with them and their three children, Melville, Elsie and Ashley, and for a short while was very happy.

His road to disaster began when he went to the theatre to watch 'May Gordon' perform on stage. Still completely smitten with the actress he decided that he needed to be financially worthy of her success and popularity and as a result embarked on a scheme to obtain money. Having been foiled in his attempts to acquire it through false representations of prestigious musical scripts, once again the 'tempter' in the form of the Devil filled his head with a solution – robbery on an express train. On 27 June 1881, armed with a revolver and a razor he arrived at London Bridge Station and purchased a one way first class ticket to Brighton.

His victim was to be Frederick Isaac Gold, a 64-year-old retired baker who was born in Clerkenwell, London in 1817. Frederick Gold lived at Titchfield House, Clermont Terrace, Preston Park in Sussex. Married to Lydia Matilda Gold née Wood for nearly 40 years, the couple had no children and had retired from the east end of London to Sussex. He was a railway season ticket holder and made regular weekly journeys to London to collect the takings from his bakery shop in Walworth, visit the bank and order flour. Percy chose him as his victim simply because he was sitting on his own in a first-class carriage and appeared to be dozing as he had a handkerchief over his face.

As the train sped along the line and entered a tunnel, Percy closed his eyes, extended his arm and pulled the trigger. Frederick Gold did not die immediately – the pair fell to the floor and embarked in a deadly struggle – Percy, urged on by fresh demons, opened the carriage door and pushed Frederick Gold to his death.

The train pulled into Preston Park Station and ticket collector, Joseph Starks, discovered Percy drenched in blood, near hysteria and asking to see a doctor. He claimed to have been attacked by a rough looking countryman who had been in the same compartment as himself and Frederick Gold. There was no sign of anyone else in the carriage and Percy suggested the two men must have jumped out. A gold watch chain was half hidden in his shoe and on suspicion of theft, he was taken to Brighton Police Station where he gave his name as Arthur Lefroy. Interviewed by the chief constable, James Terry asked him for further details of his injuries and why there was a chain hanging from his shoe. Percy maintained he had been attacked on the train and needed to see a doctor but denied any knowledge of the watch claiming it was probably his own. He was allowed to return home to seek medical attention as long as he was accompanied by two policemen, Constable Howland and Detective Sergeant Holmes. The blood-stained train compartment was shunted into sidings to await an examination by police and railway officials. Bullets were found embedded in the back of one of the seats and blood was spattered around the compartment and on the outside handle of the door.

Shortly before Percy left Brighton, two railway platelayers, Thomas Jennings and his nephew William made a gruesome discovery in the mile long Balcombe Tunnel about 20 miles north of Brighton. Frederick Gold was lying on his back, his face badly cut and covered with blood and his thumb was almost severed. His body was taken to Balcombe station and from there placed in the stables of the Railway Hotel where a local doctor pronounced that life was extinct.

A telegram was sent to London Bridge Station informing them of the death, but the news failed to reach policemen Howland or Holmes who had only just arrived at 4, Cathcart Road, Wallington with Percy Lefroy Mapleton. Leaving him in the care of his relatives – Annie Clayton was at the time in labour with her fourth child, a boy, Wilfrid Thomas Clayton, who would later take Holy Orders – the police constables began to make their way back to Brighton. When they arrived at Wallington Station, they were handed a telegram telling them to keep Percy in safe custody and not to lose sight of him. Unfortunately, by the time they returned to the house, Percy had disappeared.

On Friday 1 July 1881, newspaper history was made when for the first time it featured a picture of a wanted man. The likeness of Percy Mapleton was not good and within a short period of time more than 50 people who had nothing to do with the crime had been arrested. It was not until 8 July – 11 days after the murder – that Percy was traced to 32 Smith Street, Stepney just off the Mile End Road in London where he had taken lodgings with a middle-aged widow called Mrs Bickers.

After a short stay at Westminster police station, Percy was escorted by train from Victoria Station bound for Lewes Prison while a magistrate's enquiry was initiated. The family solicitor, Mr Dutton, who had only just finished representing his sister Mary in her divorce proceedings, travelled to see him. Percy assured him of his innocence. The enquiry lasted several days with Percy being taken by coach to Cuckfield, Sussex to hear evidence of his alleged crime. Many witnesses were called including the railway officials who had first come into contact with him and stated they believed he was a lunatic who had tried to commit suicide. The police officials were discredited in court for having allowed him to escape their custody. The only time that Percy appeared uneasy was when Frederick Gold's widow, Lydia, dressed in black, stood to give evidence that her husband was 'a very kind-hearted man, affable and pleasant in company and, so far as she knew, liked by everyone with whom he came into contact'. At the end of the enquiry, the magistrates came to the unanimous decision that Percy should stand trial at the next assizes on the capital charge of murder.

The trial began on 8 November 1881 at Maidstone Assizes, Kent before the presiding judge, John Duke, 1st Baron Coleridge. Percy was defended by one of the leading barristers of the day, Montagu Stephen Williams QC, and Sir Henry James, 1st Baron of Hereford, QC led for the prosecution. On being asked how he pleaded, Percy stated 'I plead what I am, and that is not guilty'. Despite evidence that he was insane – even his second cousin Frank Seale admitted that he did not believe Percy to be compos mentis – Percy refused to accept this as a plea. His defence team were therefore obliged to prove the existence of a third man in the railway carriage who had been responsible for the murder and Percy's injuries.

The trial was followed keenly, with people queuing each day to get a seat and listen to proceedings. Despite the brilliant oratory abilities of Montagu Williams, evidence of innocence was difficult to prove particularly as many articles of Percy's blood-stained clothes were brought into the court for the inspection of the jury. The judge's summing up speech which lasted for three hours pointed out the differences between the victim and the prisoner and left the jury in little doubt about his opinion on culpability. The jury only took ten minutes to reach their verdict and Judge Coleridge placed the black cap on his head before pronouncing the death sentence. Percy was asked if he had anything to say, and in a barely audible voice replied, 'I have only to thank the gentlemen of the jury.'

Percy was taken back to Lewes Prison where he was placed in the condemned cell – his execution was fixed to take place at nine o'clock on Tuesday 29 November 1881.

Dr Winslow attended the trial at the request of Percy's family to determine his mental state. Shortly afterwards, the press published a letter he had written explaining his findings.

'I must confess that I was surprised that the question of the responsibility of the prisoner was not raised. There is no doubt that Lefroy has a strong hereditary predisposition to insanity, his father and grandfather having both been insane. His behaviour in Court was a most strange and unnatural one, the explanation to me being either that he was indifferent to what was going on, or that he was for some reason, not yet explained, unaware of the gravity of his position.'

A petition to the Home Secretary, Sir William Vernon Harcourt, pleading for mercy and proving he was insane at the time of the murder, was compiled by his solicitor Mr Dutton using the evidence from Dr Winslow. Percy was very much against a plea of insanity despite knowing the consequences if it failed. Attached to it was evidence from the family doctor, Dr Green that Percy's mother was suffering from 'intense melancholia and paroxysm of frenzy' at the time of his birth which he believed would become hereditary. He also stated that Percy's father had become insane as a result of excessive drinking and had tried to suffocate his wife and commit suicide. The petition was signed by over 2,000 people. Unfortunately, the Home Secretary disagreed and allowed the law to take its course.

As Percy awaited the day of his execution, his family visited him on several occasions. He asked to see his young nephew Melville Clayton who was only seven years old and this was permitted by his family and the prison authorities.

In a final attempt to have his execution delayed, three days before he was due to be hanged, Percy confessed to the killing of Lieutenant Percy Lyon Ormsby Roper of the Royal Engineers at Brompton Barracks, Chatham, Kent on 11 February 1881. He later retracted this confession in an autobiography which he wrote while in the condemned cell.

With only 24 hours to go and the chance of a reprieve unlikely, William Marwood, the government's hangman since 1872, arrived at the prison and inspected the scaffold which had been specially constructed for the occasion. There was no elevated platform which had to be climbed by a ladder – the double trap door had been constructed at ground level, under which a deep pit had been dug into which the prisoner's body would drop when Marwood pulled the lever. A much smaller pit had been dug in the corner of the yard and a pile of earth was waiting to cover the coffin of the condemned man.

At 8:30 the following morning, 14 reporters were allowed to enter and were given a tour by Marwood who stated that all the arrangements were 'excellent'. He showed them the rope and noose that would be used, telling them that it was made of Italian hemp and had already been used to hang nine people the last of which was the day before in Manchester.

Percy was nearing the end of his life but slept well the night before his execution and had a light breakfast the following morning. He spent time with the prison chaplain before Marwood entered the condemned cell to pinion his arms to his body. Percy asked, 'Do you think the rope will break?' to which Marwood replied that it was quite safe. Percy walked without assistance to the gallows and stood and faced the spectators as the noose was placed around his neck and a white cap placed over his head. Marwood pulled the lever and Percy fell nine feet to his death.

In accordance with the Capital Punishment Amendment Act of 1868, an inquest into Percy's death was held shortly afterwards. Over 50 people had made applications to be part of the jury but only 14 were chosen. Captain George Augustus Crickitt, Governor of Lewes Prison, identified the body as Percy Lefroy Mapleton aged 22 years to the jurymen selected for the role. Percy's body was lying in a coffin in the prison infirmary having been left to hang for an hour in accordance with the statute. Mr Richard Turner, Surgeon of Her Majesty's Civil and Naval Prisons, Lewes, Sussex confirmed that life was extinct, death had been instantaneous and was due to judicial hanging. Percy's body was buried in the grave which had already been prepared in the precincts of the prison.

Percy left an autobiography – in which he confessed to the murder of Frederick Gold – to the prison chaplain requesting that he should make a decision whether it should be published and if he believed it should, he should liaise with Thomas Clayton of Wallington who would represent his relatives. He hoped that any proceeds would be used to pay the costs of his defence lawyers. The manuscript was passed to the Home Office who made the decision that it should not be made available for publication.

Frederick Gold's widow, Lydia, remained in the home she had shared with her husband and died on 27 February 1910. Percy's elder sister, Mary, left England with her children following Percy's execution and settled in Australia. Thomas Clayton and his wife Annie Clayton née Seale moved from Wallington to Croydon. Annie died on 14 June 1913.

A waxwork figure of Percy Lefroy Mapleton was displayed for many years in the Chamber of Horrors at Madame Tussauds in London.

Charles Taylor

Charles Taylor stood trial on two counts – murdering his wife, which was a capital offence punishable by death, and also attempting to commit suicide.

INSANE BUT HANGED

In nineteenth century England and Wales suicide was illegal. Those who tried and failed could be charged with attempted self-murder, and anyone who assisted or abetted them could also be charged as accessories to their crime. By the 1870s, an average of over 800 people a year were being arrested in England and Wales for attempted suicide, rising to over 1,000 a year in the 1890s. However, only a small percentage of those arrested were actually committed for trial. In England and Wales suicide was condemned a mortal sin in the eyes of the Church and the law. Those who succeeded were guilty of a crime known as felo de se – a felon of oneself. The implication of this was that prior to 1823 people guilty of felo de se could not receive a Christian burial in consecrated ground. The Church's view was that they had violated the Church's belief that 'Life' was a God-given gift and not for man to take away. The burial restrictions were relaxed by the 1823 Burial of Suicide Act and the 1882 Interments (felo de se) Act.

In Scotland, suicide itself was not an offence but a person attempting suicide could be charged with a 'breach of the peace' and anyone assisting a suicide could be charged with murder or culpable homicide.

Charles Taylor and his wife Caroline Elizabeth Fleming were both born in Hampshire in the early 1840s and grew up as neighbours in Portsea where they married in 1867. Their first child, a daughter named Caroline Elizabeth after her mother, was born the following year. Charles was a carpenter and joiner and hoping to find better work opportunities, the family moved to America in the early 1870s and began living in Chicago. While there, Caroline gave birth to a second child whom Charles believed not to be his. Charles later admitted that he left her and went to live alone in the Prairies but his word was uncorroborated and could not be certain to be true. However, the child died and by the mid-1870s the couple and their elder daughter returned to England and settled for a short time in Liverpool, Lancashire where another daughter, Jane Ann, was born in 1876. By 1881 the family of four were living in a shared dwelling in Peckham, London.

Charles undertook a variety of jobs with building firms but left them if he thought there were Scotsmen working on the same site as he believed them to be against him. Employers tried to be tolerant, finding him work on different sites, but Charles only lasted a few weeks before complaining about his co-workers. On one occasion, when he was working at Cavendish College, Cambridge, Charles disappeared from the site leaving his tools scattered all over the building. Discovering that he was not at his lodgings, the foreman wrote to his wife to try to discover his whereabouts because he was certain that Charles had hanged himself. His wife replied that he had walked home to London.

At the beginning of 1882, Charles spoke about wanting to take his own life and confided to a friend, John Woodhead, that 'he felt he could go home and light the copper fire and boil himself to death'. He also expressed a desire to join the Moonlighters in Ireland and do some grand deed. Employers began to avoid hiring him, believing him to be out of his mind and warnings were given to their men not to interfere with him in case he was dangerous. Charles was a member of an employment benefit society and was placed on the sick list.

By the summer of 1882, the family had moved to rented accommodation at 2, Tustin Street, Old Kent Road, London, a property that was shared with another couple, Henry and Isabel Dennington. Charles had a shop attached to his home and was a general dealer. His wife was employed more in the shop than him – he spent much of his time at home unable to work. He was affectionate towards his wife and children and, although considered a strange man by the Denningtons, the family appeared to be content. That summer, Caroline Taylor's parents, William and Jane Fleming, arrived from Portsmouth to stay with the family for several weeks. From that time, the relationship between Charles and Caroline began to deteriorate with frequent arguments and at least one physical assault which resulted in Caroline acquiring a black eye.

On 18 August, 15-year-old Caroline Elizabeth went out at lunchtime returning about an hour later. As she opened the parlour door she saw both her father and mother lying on the floor with their heads towards the fireplace and blood between them. Letting out a scream which alerted Mr and Mrs Dennington, they ran to see what had occurred. Mr Dennington immediately went for assistance, sending for both a doctor and the police.

Police Constable John Johnson was the first to arrive at the scene. Seeing Charles Taylor lying on his back with his throat cut and his wife lying by his side apparently dead, he sent for his inspector and a doctor. There was no sign of a fight and the table had been laid for a meal. The large white handled carving knife normally used to cut a joint of meat was covered in blood and had clearly been used to cut flesh of another kind.

Inspector James Levitt arrived at the house shortly after surgeon John Gordon Manwaring who had a practice on the Old Kent Road. Inspector Levitt knelt beside Charles Taylor and asked him who had committed the crime. Pointing to the carving knife, Charles admitted, 'I did, with that; she was always nagging at me.' He then lapsed into unconsciousness and was moved on to the counter in his shop where two policemen were posted to remain with him. Surgeon Manwaring confirmed that Caroline appeared to have had her throat cut from behind severing the jugular vein and the carotid artery. Charles' injuries appeared to have been self-inflicted. Charles Taylor was taken to Guy's Hospital the following day and a policeman remained with him. Charles confided to the policeman about events that day between himself and his wife:

> 'about half an hour previous to this occurred I asked my wife to turn virtuous, and that I would forgive her, as she had had a child by another man; she said, no, I will do for you yet, and sleep with another man; on that I flew at her like a madman; I did not intend to kill her, I had the knife to kill myself'.

Charles remained in hospital for nine days after which he was sufficiently well to be taken into custody and charged with the wilful murder of his wife and attempting to commit suicide. After the charge was read to him he replied, 'That is right.'

Charles Taylor was held at Newgate Prison and tried before Justice Henry Hawkins, 1st Baron Brampton, QC at the Old Bailey in a case that lasted two days in November 1882. A lot of evidence relating to his state of mind was heard in court and Dr Lyttleton Forbes Winslow and Dr John Sparkes acting surgeon of Newgate both examined him in order to form an opinion regarding his sanity.

Both Dr Winslow and Dr Sparkes questioned Charles about the motives for his crime. The transcript of the conversation was heard in court.

> "'I did the act in consequence of the adultery of my wife it was done on the impulse of the moment". Asked whether he and his wife had been on friendly terms together he said "Yes". Asked if he could mention any single individual with whom he could accuse his wife of infidelity; he said "No". Asked on what grounds he arrived at the conclusion as to the adultery he said "from certain observations which she made occasionally". Asked to illustrate what he meant, and after thinking a few seconds he said that one day while at the theatre with his wife she exclaimed, alluding to one of the actors on the stage, "What a fine-looking man that is". I returned home and imagined that that actor had been carrying on intrigues with my wife.

Questioned as to his wonderful powers of cure; he said that he was able to cure all diseases, and that his attention was always absorbed in considering the ways and manners of society, that he had visited the South Kensington Museum, and had seen there the bust of Oliver Cromwell, and in consequence of the similarity existing between it and himself he was destined to be as great a man in history as Oliver Cromwell had been. He informed me that he was jealous and suspicious, and never could get on with his fellow-workmen because they were always complaining against him, that he had suffered very much from want of sleep, and frequently during the night he would get up and wander about the room, that he had contemplated committing suicide on several occasions, but had never made any actual attempt to destroy himself.'

Dr Winslow was cross-examined by Mr Greenwood, the prisoner's Counsel, who had requested him as a witness in order to determine and explain to the court the mental condition of Charles Taylor. Dr Winslow provided the court with the following statement of his findings:

'I attend here today for the purpose of seeing a man who was supposed to be insane, and who was going to be tried for murder. I do not think he knew who I was, and I did not tell him. I conversed with him about twenty minutes at each time, and that was quite sufficient for me to say that he is of unsound mind. He certainly knows that he is on trial for the murder of his wife, and that it is necessary for him to defend himself on that charge, and to excuse himself for it and explain it, but I do not think he had the least idea that I was examining him to test his mental condition. I do not think he has sufficient sense to make suggestions for his defence. I said "had you any reason for committing the act?" I did not say what act, he knew perfectly well that I meant the act of killing his wife. I think I said "motive" not "reason" and I think he said "I committed the murder in consequence of the adultery of my wife". I did not conclude from that that he was insane I believe he suspected her, and that there was no cause for it. Being suspicious without proper cause is not evidence of insanity, taken by itself. Perfectly sane men often have a suspicion of their wives having committed adultery. If he had a suspicion of it that would be a motive for his being angry with her, so that there is nothing in that, nor is there anything in his statement that he had the power of curing all diseases he might be merely a vain quack boasting of his power. I do not see any sign of insanity in that. I consider that his saying that he was destined to be as great a man as Oliver Cromwell is a sign of insanity. If he fancied he could cure diseases which other people could not, and so make a great man of himself in his own imagination, I should consider him more insane, and if he believed he could do it that would increase his insanity. I decidedly mean to represent that as cogent evidence of insanity. I attribute importance to his jealousy and suspicion, with the other symptoms of muttering to himself, and the ideas of greatness. I have known plenty of sane men who have not committed suicide, but who have attempted to. I do not believe that every man who attempts to take his own life is insane; it is not evidence of insanity by itself. I also base my opinion on his idea that people were plotting against him so that he could not get on with his work. I thoroughly believe that he attacked his wife and killed her because he suspected she had committed adultery, and that he took her life to punish her for her misconduct; it is a very common form of innocent suspicion. My opinion is that he is of unsound mind decidedly.

'I asked him if he was conscious of the position he was in, and he began to cry, but did not answer the question at all. I asked him whether he could give me another illustration of anything his wife said which made him jealous. He said one night she woke up and said that she felt her heart shake in her body, and he believed there was some man who she had been carrying on an intrigue with. I have sometimes seen persons suspect upon grounds which are ridiculously absurd. I asked him what his mind chiefly dwelt upon. He said upon the habits and appearances of people, their size, and the colour of their eyes, and those facts had occupied his mind for years. I asked him whether he was interested in what went on in the world. He said "no", his attention was only occupied with those subjects'.

Dr John Sparkes agreed that when Charles Taylor had committed the murder of his wife he had been insane. He also told the court that he had seen no evidence of insanity while he had been a prisoner at Newgate and he had seen him on a daily basis. Dr George Henry Savage, resident physician of Bethlehem and a lecturer on mental diseases at Guy's Hospital, also examined Charles Taylor while he was in hospital recovering from the wound to his neck. As he had attempted to commit suicide as well as murdering his wife, he felt it important to see him to ascertain his state of mind. Dr Savage discovered no signs of insanity and Charles answered his questions with no hesitation. Charles admitted that he had had a head injury many years previously as a result of falling from a great height when he was a shipwright. He also stated that an uncle was insane. It is likely that the evidence from these two doctors swayed the jury who after a short deliberation found Charles Taylor guilty of wilful murder. The court stated that 'a man may be sane on some matters and insane on others – a partial insanity may exist –violent suspicion is a common symptom of insanity, but not a decisive test'. The death sentence was passed.

Charles was removed to HM Prison Wandsworth to await his execution. Following his conviction, he expressed penitence for the crime. A request for clemency was made to the Home Secretary but he failed to intervene and the law duly took its course. The night before the execution, Charles was visited by two of his brothers for the last time. After a restless night, at 9 am on Tuesday 12 December 1882, looking very pale and ill, he walked without assistance to the scaffold. William Marwood, who had hanged Percy Lefroy Mapleton almost exactly 12 months previously was in attendance. Marwood was responsible for introducing 'the long drop' method of hanging to England. He determined that if the prisoner was to be given a drop of between six to ten feet depending on his weight and with the noose correctly positioned, death would be fairly instantaneous due to the neck being broken. The long drop removed the gruesome struggling and convulsing of prisoners hanging from the noose and was undoubtedly, less cruel to the prisoner and far less distressing to the prison staff who were obliged to witness the proceedings at close quarters.

Marwood allowed a drop of over eight feet for Charles Taylor and the condemned man appeared to die without a struggle. At the inquest following the execution, necessary by law to ensure that procedures had taken place in the correct manner, the jurymen reasonably asked why Charles Taylor's head appeared to have been severed from his body. Dr Winter, the prison surgeon, explained that although the wound to his throat from his attempted suicide had healed, the scar tissue was delicate.

Marwood's use of the 'long drop' had re-opened the damaged tissue and the extensive haemorrhage that had occurred during the execution was no more than could be expected from death by a fracture of the vertebrae and rupture of the vessels of the neck. There were very few people present outside the prison when the black flag was raised and the notification of execution was posted on the gate. Whether his two daughters were waiting outside is unclear. Like Percy Mapleton, Charles Taylor was buried within the prison walls.

People were disturbed in their conscience that individuals doomed to be executed who were not responsible for their actions at the time their crimes took place should be cured by a noose instead of a strait jacket. There had been other cases such as the murder of Caroline Sophia Colborne by George Broomfield and his attempted suicide in 1864 which had created much debate in the press about the question of sanity and insanity. Sentenced to hang, George Broomfield had his sentence commuted to penal servitude for life.

Medical understanding of insanity was in its infancy in nineteenth century Britain. More than one doctor was obliged to sign a certificate for admission to an asylum and in the courtroom, more than one doctor provided medical evidence to explain to judge and jury their reasoned opinion on the mental health of the prisoner. If the opinions of doctors, however eminent differed, then the jury were obliged to come to their own conclusions and determine the fate of the accused. Juries often requested leniency of the judge before he passed sentence, but this was not always respected. The press were eager to point out to their readers that a Court of Appeal in cases of murder would be a definite advantage.

Towards the latter end of the nineteenth century, the legal system underwent a period of change and the Judicature Act of 1873 introduced the Court of Appeal for civil cases. Although criminal appeal rights remained limited until the establishment of a Court of Criminal Appeal in 1907, there existed a higher authority should prisoners wish to question their sentence. Had the same court existed at the time John Bellingham was convicted of murder in 1812, he would not have been executed within a week of judgement being passed against him.

Radical change had also taken place in the provision of care and treatment of both the mentally ill and the criminally insane. Manacles and chains had been replaced by therapy and care for those unfortunate enough to suffer from 'insanity' at a time when little could be done to relieve it. In many ways, the nineteenth century could be seen as a period of enlightenment and improvement. It provided the basis of judicial reform which remains in existence to this day and built provision for the criminally insane which is still in use.

Appendix

Asylum Medical Superintendents

Broadmoor

Dr John Meyer

John Meyer was born in 1814 at Norwood, Surrey. He qualified as a Doctor of Medicine at the University of Heidelberg, Baden-Württemberg, Germany in 1836. Marrying Emma Shuttleworth in December 1839 in Bishop Tawton, Devon, the couple had eight children. Meyer applied for employment as a British Colonial Surgeon and was sent to Van Diemen's Land, Australia, in 1841, which was the main British penal colony at that time. In 1844, Meyer was appointed Medical Superintendent of the Hospital and Convict Lunatic Asylum at New Norfolk. This asylum was built in 1827 following the separation of Van Diemen's Land from New South Wales. (Until 1825 New South Wales with Van Diemen's Land had been considered a single Colony. They divided into two separate Colonies in 1825. In 1856, Van Diemen's Land became known as 'Tasmania').

The New Norfolk Asylum was built to house invalid and lunatic convicts who had been transported from England. The asylum was expanded in 1830 through the hard and harsh law of Lieutenant Governor George Arthur (1784-1854). In Meyer's time, there would have been about 130 inmates strictly controlled under Arthur's military style rule of law.

After Meyer's return to England, his talent for organisation was recognised and the Government appointed him to form, establish and run the new British civilian hospital at Smyrna (Izmir) in Turkey during the Crimean War. They were much impressed by the way he conducted his services, and on his return to England he was appointed Chief Resident Physician to the Surrey Lunatic Asylum at Tooting. Meyer was then appointed in 1862 to be the first medical superintendent of the Criminal Lunatic Asylum at Broadmoor, of which he was an organiser, taking up his post the following year.

In his duty to classify lunatics under various headings and to develop a better understanding of insanity, Meyer grouped the inmates according to their crimes, perceived causes of insanity, occupation, degree of education, and his opinion on their chances of recovery. He overestimated the recovery rate as one in six – during his tenure of office only one in twenty of his patients recovered sufficiently to be released.

Dr John Meyer was attacked by a patient, John Hughes, in March 1866 and received a very ugly wound to the right side of the head, the effects of which he felt till his death a few years later. He died suddenly on 9 May 1870 in Exeter, Devon, aged 56 years. He was buried at Norwood Cemetery, Lambeth, London on 12 May 1870. He had four sons and four daughters, but only one son and two daughters survived him. His widow was awarded a Civil List Pension from the Crown of £60 a year 'in consideration of the services of her late husband as Superintendent of the Hospital at Smyrna during the Crimean War and afterwards of the Criminal Lunatic Asylum at Broadmoor'. At the time of his death, Broadmoor had reached the capacity for its accommodation with 400 male and 100 female criminal lunatics.

Dr William Orange

Dr William Orange succeeded Dr John Meyer as the second medical superintendent of Broadmoor in May 1870. He was of Huguenot extraction, descending from an ancestor who settled in Chesterfield, Derbyshire in the seventeenth century. William was born in Newcastle-upon-Tyne, Northumberland on 24 October 1834, the son of the Reverend John Orange, an Independent Baptist minister, and his wife Martha Edge (d. 1861). Shortly afterwards, due to Martha's ill-health, the family moved to Torquay, Devon where John Orange took charge of the Union Church in Chapel Street, Tormoham. William Orange flourished at school in Torquay and when he was 15 years old he was apprenticed to a doctor at Swallowfield, Berkshire to learn the arts and crafts of medicine. He subsequently studied at St Thomas's Hospital in London, and graduated there in 1856 as a Member of the Royal College of Surgeons of England and a Licentiate of the Society of Apothecaries of London. After graduation, he embarked on a prolonged tour of Europe in charge of a gentleman who had suffered a mental breakdown, and he welcomed the opportunity to travel, learning French, German, and Italian – a gift he cherished in future years.

APPENDIX: ASYLUM MEDICAL SUPERINTENDENTS

After returning to England and working temporarily in a dispensary in Portland Town, London, William Orange spent three years as the Assistant Medical Officer at the Surrey County Lunatic Asylum at Tooting under the supervision of Dr John Meyer. Orange was appointed Deputy Superintendent at Broadmoor when it opened, starting in his post there in November 1862 on the recommendation of, and under Meyer. William Orange married Florence Elizabeth Hart on 12 April 1864 at St Marylebone, Middlesex. In 1868, he was awarded the degree of Doctor of Medicine from Heidelberg University and was subsequently elected a Fellow of the Royal College of Physicians of London in 1878.

As Medical Superintendent, Orange took a more liberal approach than Meyer and was a proponent of social integration and encouraged arts, crafts, sports and evening entertainments as part of the patients' rehabilitation. Books and newspapers were provided to give 'mental occupation and education' to the patients. Cricket was played enthusiastically in the summer months. Working parties were introduced to encourage patients to work together in market gardening in the estate around Broadmoor. Orange earned a world-wide reputation as an authority on the treatment of criminal lunatics. He was a methodical man and excelled in organisation, turning Broadmoor into a well-run institution. Orange renewed Dr Meyer's complaints to the Home Office about the excessive number of disruptive 'lunatic convicts' in Broadmoor compared to those patients detained at 'Her Majesty's pleasure'. Public opinion was roused when four convict inmates managed to escape from Broadmoor in 1873 – two of whom were never recaptured – one was a murderer, William Bisgrove, an illegitimate epileptic of 'feeble-mind' who, intoxicated with beer in August 1868, when only 19 years of age, allegedly bashed out the brains of a sleeping navvy working on the Cheddar Valley Railway in Somerset by dropping a heavy stone on his head three or four times. In view of these Broadmoor escapes and the representations of the medical superintendents, the government took action and in 1875 most of the 'lunatic convicts' were moved from Broadmoor to Woking Invalid Prison at Knaphill in Surrey where a special wing had been built to receive them – it was also designed by Sir Joshua Jebb (the architect of Broadmoor), but closed in 1886 when many convict lunatics were returned to Broadmoor.

William Orange was elected President of the Medico-Psychological Society in 1883-84. In his presidential address, he explained his appreciation concerning the relationship of mental derangement to the law. He criticised the term 'criminal lunatic' on the grounds 'that it was a contradiction: one could not be both guilty of crime and be a lunatic, since the latter could not, by definition, be held criminally responsible'.

The most noteworthy change that Orange brought about to the daily management of Broadmoor was a system of rewarding the inmates for the effort they put in into the workshops. Prior to 1874, inmates could be rewarded for working with two glasses of beer a day and cheese for lunch. In 1874, payment by results was instituted. Patients were allowed to spend one-eighth of the estimated value of their produce to purchase small luxuries. The output from the tailor and shoemaker shops immediately doubled.

On 6 June 1882, Dr William Orange was attacked by a patient, Rev Henry John Dodwell during a private meeting at Dodwell's request. Dodwell struck Dr Orange forcibly on the temple with a stone wrapped in a handkerchief. Orange was badly hurt, but managed to escape the room out into the corridor where staff came to his rescue.

The strain of work after his head injury had weakened Orange, and reduced his stamina and confidence making him consider and reflect on his situation. He retired as medical superintendent of Broadmoor in 1886 but did provide further valuable service using his knowledge and experience to become a member of Broadmoor's Council of Supervision from 1892 until 1904. In Queen Victoria's Birthday Honours List of June 1886 Orange was created a Companion of the Civil Division of the Most Honourable Order of the Bath (CB).

William and Florence had four daughters and a son. One of their daughters, Margaret Orange, born in 1869 at Broadmoor, graduated in medicine as a Licentiate of the Society of Apothecaries of London in 1896 and served as the Assistant Medical Officer at Claybury Asylum at Woodford Bridge in Essex. Their son, Sir Hugh William Orange, KBE, CB, CIE, was Director General of Education in India from 1906-11 and then Accountant-General of the Board of Education in England, 1911-28. William Orange died at Bexhill-on-Sea, Sussex on 31 December 1916, aged 82 years. His wife predeceased him by three years.

Dr David Nicolson

The third medical superintendent of Broadmoor was Dr David Nicolson who was born on Christmas Day 1844 in Auchlethen, Cruden, Aberdeenshire, the son of William Nicolson, a coal merchant, and his wife Catherine Simpson.

He graduated Bachelor of Medicine (with honours) and Master of Surgery from the University of Aberdeen in 1866, and as Doctor of Medicine in 1875. He worked as the Medical Officer at the prisons of Woking, Portland and Millbank from 1867 until 1873 and as Senior Medical Officer at Portsmouth Prison until 1876 when he was appointed Deputy Medical Superintendent at Broadmoor. In 1883, during his time as Deputy, he was assaulted by a patient, Henry Forrester who had been admitted to Broadmoor on 16 July 1880 following an assault on a hospital doctor in London.

Dr David Nicolson married Edith Margaret Case at Fareham, Hampshire in October 1886 and succeeded William Orange as medical superintendent of Broadmoor in the same year. He was injured by another patient, James Lyons, who threw a stone striking him on the head in 1889, cutting his scalp and laying him up with concussion for ten weeks.

Nicolson served on the Home Office Department Committee on Habitual Drunkards, 1891-92, and the Irish Government Committee of Inquiry into Dundrum Criminal Lunatic Asylum, 1891 and he chaired the Irish Departmental Committee on Insanity amongst Convicts, 1904. He was President of the Medico-Psychological Association (MPA), 1895-96. His presidential address on 'Crime, Criminals, and Criminal Lunatics' robustly rejected the notion of criminal anthropology or phrenology.

On retiring from Broadmoor in 1895, Hardridge Stanley Giffard, 1st Earl of Halsbury, the Lord Chancellor, appointed Nicolson as one of his Visitors in Lunacy. In a break from tradition, his deputy, Dr John Baldwin Isaac, was not selected to succeed him, and the post of medical superintendent went to Richard Brayn.

The family appear on the 1911 Census at Blytheswood, London Road, Frimley, Surrey. David Nicolson stated his occupation as Lord Chancellor's Visitor in Lunacy, Civil Service. He was living with his wife, Edith Margaret, and their three daughters, Alice Margaret, Maud Morshead and Edith Haig Nicolson, and two servants. David Nicolson died on 28 June 1932 in Camberley, Surrey and was buried at St Peter's, Frimley, Surrey.

Sir Richard Brayn

Richard Brayn was born at Market Drayton, Shropshire on 14 June 1850, son of Joseph George Brayn and his wife Louisa Spalding. He was educated privately at home, then at Wem Grammar School before entering King's College, London in 1870.

Brayn became a Member of the Royal College of Surgeons of England in 1873, and a Licentiate of the Royal College of Physicians of London in 1874. He travelled to South Africa in 1875. On his return to England, he entered the Prison Service and was appointed assistant surgeon to Portsmouth Prison, subsequently becoming assistant surgeon to HM Prison at Millbank. In 1879, he was appointed medical officer at HM Prison, Pentonville. His abilities in this more responsible charge were recognised and he was promoted to be medical officer of HM Prison, Woking in 1882 which was considered at that time to be the invalid convict prison, but also gave him charge of what were called 'the insane convicts'. In 1889, he became governor and medical officer of the female convict prison there.

Brayn was keen to explore mental illnesses especially when they were connected with criminality. He had a long background and considerable experience as a prison doctor and he knew how to treat criminals rather than lunatics. He displayed shrewd common sense. It was unsurprising that Brayn was appointed medical superintendent of Broadmoor from 1898 until 1910. He received much commendation and admiration for the way Broadmoor was run under his superintendence although he was noted to use seclusion (solitary confinement) more regularly than any of his predecessors.

Richard Brayn was knighted in 1911 on the occasion of George V's Coronation shortly after his retirement in recognition of the work he had done at Broadmoor, and in the same year he was appointed a Home Office Expert in Lunacy. He died after a short illness at Gledholt, Hereford Road, Southsea-on-Sea, Hampshire on 12 March 1912. He was survived by his wife Laura Jane (née Negus), daughter of the Deputy Inspector-General Fysher Negus, RN, and one son and a daughter.

Criminal Lunatic Department, Perth General Prison

John McNaughtan

John McNaughtan was born in 1851 in Perth, the son of William McNaughtan, a draper, and his wife Jessie Kinnear. He graduated as a Licentiate of the Royal College of Surgeons of Edinburgh in 1873 and went on to study at the University of Glasgow where he obtained the degrees of Bachelor of Medicine (with commendation) in 1875, and Doctor of Medicine in 1877. After a brief spell as a ship's surgeon, he became Assistant and District Surgeon to the Perth County and City Infirmary. By 1880 he had been appointed Resident Medical Officer at the Criminal Lunatic Department at the General Prison, Perth and lived in a house within the prison site, South View. In 1885, McNaughtan became the Department's Medical Superintendent. The 1891 Census records John McNaughtan living at South View with his widowed mother together with a cook and a general servant.

On 8 October 1892, John McNaughtan, then 41-years-old, married his first wife, 24-year-old Janie Taylor whose residence was given as Barlinnie Prison, Hogganfield Parish, Glasgow. Janie was the daughter of the prison governor, James Taylor and Jane Crick. John and Janie had two daughters, Jessie Kinnear McNaughtan and Jean Crick McNaughtan.

In 1901, an annexe to the Criminal Lunatic Asylum at Perth was opened to house the Scottish State Inebriate Reformatory. This provision was created following the Inebriates Act of 1898 which was designed to address the problems of the increasing number of criminal acts committed by habitual drunkards, particularly in the lower classes of society. Not only was alcoholism being considered a disease in its own right, but other possible illnesses resulting from habitual drinkers' lifestyles might require admission to an institution with a medical facility. John McNaughtan took on the added responsibility for this provision at Perth. See Chapter 7 on Mentally Weak Habitual Criminals for more information.

In the Birthday Honours List of Edward VII in November 1902, John McNaughtan was amongst the first ever Companions of the newly established Imperial Service Order – established in recognition of long and meritorious service for members of the Civil Service of the Empire.

He resigned from his post in Perth in 1908 following the death of his wife. When he did so, the post of Medical Superintendent of the Criminal Lunatic Department was made obsolete and the Medical Officer for Perth Prison was given the added responsibility of managing the Criminal Lunatic Department and the Inebriate Reformatory.

John McNaughtan married his second wife, Catherine Anne Clarke, 20 years his junior, in September 1910 in Glasgow. She was the daughter of another prison governor, William Clarke, and Helen Craik. They had one daughter, Helen Craik McNaughtan, born in October 1911. He died eight months later on 25 July 1912, aged 61 years, in Kinnoull, Perth from spastic paralysis and cardiac failure

Bibliography

ANDREWS, Jonathan; BRIGGS, Asa; PORTER, Roy; TUCKER, Penny and **WADDINGTON, Keir** (eds.), *The history of Bedlam,* (London & New York, Routledge, 1997).

BENTLEY, David *'She-Butchers: Baby-Droppers, Baby-Sweaters, and Baby-Farmers' in Rowbotham, Judith and Stevenson, Kim (eds) Criminal Conversations: Victorian Crimes, Social Panic and Moral Outrage* (Columbus: The Ohio State University Press 2005).

BURTINSHAW, Kathryn and **BURT, John**, *Lunatics, imbeciles and idiots: a history of insanity in nineteenth century Britain & Ireland,* (Barnsley: Pen & Sword, 2017).

CHARLESWORTH, Lorie, *Welfare's forgotten past: a socio-legal history of the Poor Law,* (Abingdon: Routledge, 2010).

GARDNER, James, *The trail of the serpent: the true story of a Victorian murder on the London-to-Brighton railway line,* (Lewes: Pomegranate Press, 2004).

HAWKINGS, David T., *Criminal Ancestors: a guide to historical criminal records in England and Wales,* (Stroud: The History Press, 2009).

JAY, Mike, *The way madness lies: the asylum and beyond,* (London: Thames & Hudson/Wellcome Collection, 2016).

MARLAND, Hilary, *Dangerous motherhood: Insanity and childbirth in Victorian Britain,* Basingstoke, Palgrave Macmillan, 2004).

MELLING, Joseph and **FORSYTHE, Bill** (eds.), *Insanity, institutions and society, 1800-1914: A social history of madness in comparative perspective,* (London and New York: Routlege, 1999).

PARRY-JONES, William Llywelyn, *The trade in lunacy: a study of private madhouses in England in the eighteenth and nineteenth centuries,* (London: Routledge & Kegan Paul; Toronto: University of Toronto Press, 1972).

PARTRIDGE, Ralph, *Broadmoor: a history of criminal lunacy and its problems,* (London: Chatto & Windus, 1953).

PRIOR, Pauline M., *Madness and murder: gender, crime and mental disorder in nineteenth-century Ireland,* (Dublin: Irish Academic Press, 2008).

QUINTON, Richard Frith, *Crime and Criminals,* (London: Longmans, Green and Co., 1910).

BIBLIOGRAPHY

ROWBOTHAM, Judith and **STEVENSON, Kim** (eds.), *Criminal conversations: Victorian crimes, social panic, and moral outrage,* (Columbus: The Ohio State University Press, 2005).

SCOTTISH LUNACY COMMISSION, *Report by Her Majesty's Commissioners appointed to inquire into the state of lunatic asylums in Scotland and existing law in reference to lunatics and lunatic asylums in that part of the United Kingdom,* (Edinburgh: HMSO, 1857).

SHOWALTER, Elaine, *The female malady: Women, madness and English culture, 1830-1980,* (London: Virago Press, 1987).

SMITH, Roger, '*The boundary between insanity and criminal responsibility in nineteenth-century England'* in Skull, Andrew (ed.) *Madhouses, mad-doctors, and madmen,* (Philadelphia: University of Pennsylvania Press, 1981, pp. 363-84).

STEVENS, Mark, *Broadmoor revealed: Victorian crime and the lunatic asylum,* (Barnsley: Pen & Sword, 2013).

STIRLING, Jeanette, *Representing epilepsy: Myth and matter,* (Liverpool: Liverpool University Press, 2010).

WISE, Sarah, *Inconvenient people: Lunacy, liberty and the mad-doctors in Victorian England,* (London: Vintage Books, 2013).

WRIGHT, David and **DIGBY, Anne**, (eds.), *From idiocy to mental deficiency: Historical perspectives on people with learning disabilities,* (London and New York: Routledge, 1996).

Index

INDEX